Wonders

CALIFORNIA Content Reader

English Language Development

B

The McGraw·Hill Companies

 Macmillan/McGraw-Hill

Published by Macmillan/McGraw-Hill, of McGraw-Hill Education, a division of The McGraw-Hill Companies, Inc., Two Penn Plaza, New York, New York 10121.

Printed in the United States of America

8 9 10 WEB 14 13 12

Contents

California Science Standards

Contents

Circuits

An **electric current** is a flow of electrical charges. Electric current keeps charges moving. It is like water moving in a river.

Electric current needs to flow along a path. This path is called a **circuit**. A simple circuit has three basic parts. One part is a power source, such as a battery. This powers a load, such as a bulb or a computer. Connectors, such as wires, carry electrical charges between the power source and the load.

Many circuits have a switch. A switch turns electric current on and off. A switch turns on lights in your classroom.

Charges can only keep moving if a circuit does not have breaks. A complete, unbroken circuit is called a closed circuit.

A circuit that has a break is called an open circuit. Electric current cannot flow in an open circuit. There is an open circuit when a light bulb burns out. A wire inside the bulb breaks in two parts.

Electric current helps light up Los Angeles.

All electrical charges flow in the same direction in a **series circuit**. They all flow along one path.

The parts of a series circuit are connected in one loop. The electric current moves from the power source through the wires. It moves to one load. Then it moves through another load. Finally, the current returns to the power source.

Electric current flows through more than one path in a **parallel circuit**. These different paths are called branches. The branches divide the electric current. Some of the electric current flows through each branch.

Series Circuit

This is a series circuit. The parts are connected like links in a chain. Electric current passes through each part, one at a time. If one part of the series circuit breaks, electric current cannot flow. ▶

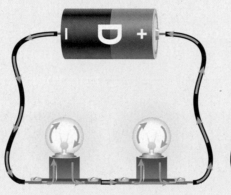

Parallel Circuit

This is a parallel circuit. Each branch is its own path. Electric current passes through each path at the same time. If one branch breaks, current will still flow through the other branches. ▶

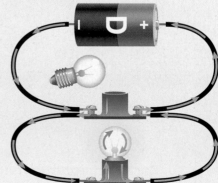

Earth's Magnetic Field

Earth's magnetic field keeps humans and animals from getting lost.

A magnetic field surrounds Earth. It helps humans and animals from getting lost. Scientists think this magnetic field starts deep inside Earth, in its core. Hot, liquid iron is constantly moving there because Earth spins and because of forces inside Earth's core. Scientists believe that this hot, moving metal is like a huge magnet inside Earth.

The magnetic field is not very strong on the surface of Earth. But it is what makes compasses work. Inside each compass is a magnetized needle. One end of the needle is pointed or painted red. This is the "north-seeking" end. The needle can turn easily. This north-seeking end is attracted to the north end of Earth's magnetic field. Early explorers who knew this could find their way. They could make maps, too.

Roger Harris/Photo Researchers, Inc.

Image Source

▲ The needle on a compass points north.

▲ The curved lines show Earth's magnetic field.

Harald Sund/Getty Images

▲ Migrating birds use Earth's magnetic field to find their way.

When North Becomes South

Imagine you traveled back in time to 80 million years ago. You looked at your compass — and you got lost! Back then, the north-seeking needle on your compass pointed south. This happened because the Earth's magnetic field was reversed. Earth's magnetic field can change.

Earth's magnetic field reverses completely about every 250,000 years. This has happened many times in Earth's history. It will probably happen again. This change can take hundreds of thousands of years. Big changes in Earth's magnetic field may make it hard for humans and animals to find their way home. —*Lisa Jo Rudy*

Solar Interference

Heat and light from the Sun make life possible on Earth. However, sometimes the Sun can cause problems.

The Sun is a fiery ball of gas. Solar flares happen on the Sun's surface. They are bursts of energy that shoot far into space. Sunspots are cooler patches on the surface. They form where the Sun's magnetic field is very strong.

Every 11 years, the number of solar flares and sunspots increases. They can affect Earth's magnetic field. It can disrupt our communications systems. Astronauts in orbit can be harmed.

SOHO-EIT Consortium/ESA/NASA

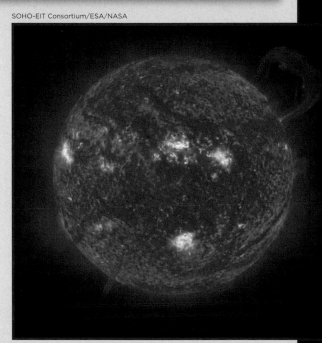

▲ Solar flares and sunspots can cause problems on Earth.

Cause/Effect Writing Frame

Use the Writing Frame to summarize "Circuits."

An electric current must have a path so that _____

_____ .

A circuit has three parts. They are _____

_____ .

If any part of a series circuit breaks, the circuit is open. **As a result,** _____

_____

_____ .

In a parallel circuit, each branch _____

_____ .

Therefore, if any branch of a parallel circuit breaks, _____

_____ .

Use the Writing Frame to write the summary on another sheet of paper. Be sure to include the **bold** signal words. Keep this as a model of this Text Structure.

Critical Thinking

1 A complete, unbroken circuit is called a _____.

    A. open circuit

    B. series circuit

    C. closed circuit

2 Find the paragraph in "Earth's Magnetic Field" that explains how a compass works.

3 Find the paragraph in "Earth's Magnetic Field" that tells how often Earth's magnetic field reverses.

4 What do the diagrams on page 7 in "Circuits" show you? Discuss this with a partner.

Diagrams are pictures that show how things relate to one another.

Digital Learning

For a list of links and activities that relate to this Science standard, visit the California Treasures Website at www.macmillanmh.com to access the Content Reader resources.

Have students view the e-Review "Electric Circuits."

In addition, distribute copies of the Translated Concept Summaries in Spanish, Chinese, Hmong, Khmer, and Vietnamese.

Electromagnets

In the 1820s and 1830s, scientists discovered that electric currents make magnetic fields. They also discovered that magnets can make an electric current.

Electric current flows through a wire. It makes a magnetic field around this wire. If you increase the current, the magnetic field gets stronger. You can also make the magnetic field stronger if you wind the wire into a long coil. Each loop of wire acts like a little magnet. The loops all push and pull in the same direction.

An **electromagnet** is a coil of wire wrapped around a metal core, such as an iron bar. Electric current flows through the coil and sets up a very strong magnetic field. The metal core then becomes magnetic. If the current stops, the metal core is not magnetic anymore.

Electromagnets and permanent magnets produce magnetic fields. A permanent magnet cannot be turned on and off. However, an electromagnet can. You simply turn the electric current on and off. You can also change the current to make the electromagnetic stronger or weaker.

▲ Electric current flows in these wires. Now the metal bar is a magnet.

You can find electromagnets in hundreds of things. They are in electric guitars and electric generators. They are in the electric motors of trains. They are also in vacuum cleaners and dishwashers.

Electromagnets are important parts of loudspeakers. You can find loudspeakers in televisions and headphones. A **loudspeaker** changes electrical energy into sound. Objects in the loudspeaker produce sound when they vibrate.

A stereo can send electric current to an electromagnet in the loudspeaker. The electromagnet is connected to a diaphragm. The diaphragm is a part of the loudspeaker. It vibrates to produce sound. Here's how it works.

▲Headphones are small loudspeakers. They have tiny electromagnets.

The loudspeaker also has a permanent magnet. When electric current flows, the permanent magnet pushes and pulls the electromagnet. As the electromagnet moves, the diaphragm moves. The moving diaphragm produces sound.

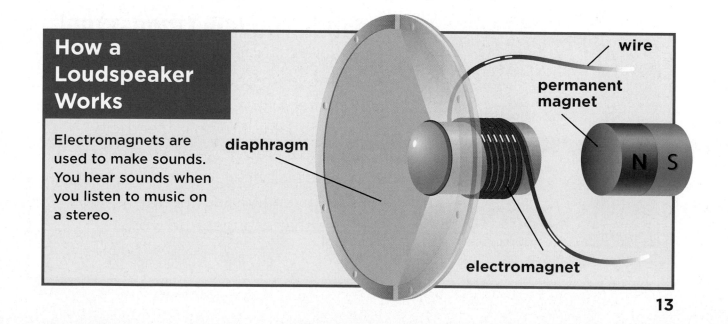

How a Loudspeaker Works

Electromagnets are used to make sounds. You hear sounds when you listen to music on a stereo.

wire

permanent magnet

diaphragm

N S

electromagnet

INVENTORS ELECTRIFY OUR WORLD

Here's a look at some scientists who helped light up our world.

Thomas Edison and his workers invented the light bulb, the phonograph, and other electrical devices. Other inventors worked with electricity, too.

Bettmann/Corbis

William Gilbert (1544-1603)

In the 1500s, William Gilbert was an Englishman who experimented with electricity. He invented the names *electricity*, *magnetic pole*, and *electric attraction*. Gilbert was the first person to discover how a magnetic compass works.

The Granger Collection

Benjamin Franklin (1706-1790)

In the 1750s and 60s, Benjamin Franklin was a famous American who also experimented with electricity. He discovered that lightning is electricity. He also discovered how to produce a kind of electricity called static electricity. Franklin's inventions led the way to later inventions that changed the world.

Hulton-Deutsch Collection/Corbis

Michael Faraday (1791-1867)

Michael Faraday was a scientist and inventor. He heard that another scientist used electricity to make a magnet. Faraday was inspired. Soon after, he invented the electric motor. He found how to make an electric current and bring electricity into our homes.

Courtesy Queens Borough Library

Lewis Latimer (1848-1928)

In the 1870s, Thomas Edison was trying to invent an electric light bulb. The businessman Hiram Maxim was trying to invent a light bulb, too. Then Maxim met Lewis Latimer, a draftsman and inventor. Latimer helped Maxim solve his problem. Latimer invented a long-lasting light bulb. After that, electricity was used to light homes and streets.

Bettmann/Corbis

Grace Hopper (1906-1992)

The first electronic computer was invented in the 1940s. In 1952, Grace Hopper was a computer scientist who invented the first computer software that helped people "talk" to computers. It was called Common Business-Oriented Language. "COBOL" became the most popular business computing language in the world.

Compare/Contrast Writing Frame

Use the Writing to orally summarize "Electromagnets."

An electromagnet is _____

_____.

Both electromagnets and permanent magnets _____

_____.

Unlike permanent magnets, electromagnets _____

_____.

Also, by changing the current, you can _____

_____.

Electromagnets can be found in _____

_____.

Use the Writing Frame to write the summary on another sheet of paper. Be sure to include the **bold** signal words. Keep this as a model of this Text Structure.

Critical Thinking

1 If an electromagnet receives more current, it _____ .

    A. becomes weaker

    B. becomes stronger

    C. turns off

2 Find the paragraph in "Inventors Electrify Our World" that tells about the light bulb. Who invented a long-lasting bulb?

3 Find the section in "Electrifying Inventors" that tells about Grace Hopper.

4 What does the diagram "How a Loudspeaker Works" on page 13 tell you? Discuss this with a partner.

> Diagrams are pictures that show how things relate to one another.

Digital Learning

For a list of links and activities that relate to this Science standard, visit the California Treasures Web site at www.macmillanmh.com to access the Content Reader resources.

Have students view the e-Review "Electromagnets."

In addition, distribute copies of the Translated Concept Summaries in Spanish, Chinese, Hmong, Khmer, and Vietnamese.

Electricity

There are different kinds of electricity. But all electricity is the result of electrical charges. **Electrical charge** is a property of matter, just like color and hardness. Everything around you is made of matter—air, water, and even this book.

There are two types of electrical charges. These charges are called positive and negative. You cannot see or feel electrical charge the way you can see color or feel hardness. However, you can observe how charges affect each other. Two positive charges repel each other. They push each other away. Two negative charges also repel each other. A positive charge and a negative charge attract each other. They pull toward each other.

▲ There are charged particles in the girl's hair. They are attracted to the charged balloon.

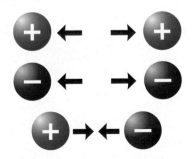

▲ Two positive (+) charges repel each other. Negative charges do this, too. Opposite charges attract each other.

Electrical currents are the flow of electrical charges. These currents carry the energy that people depend on to cook food and use computers. Electrical objects can change their energy into other kinds of energy, such as heat, light, and motion.

For example, electrical energy can be changed into heat. People use this heat to cook food, heat homes, and dry objects. Electric current passes through wires inside a hair dryer. These wires slow down the current and heat the air inside the hair dryer.

Electrical energy can light buildings and streets. An incandescent bulb produces heat and light. Inside an incandescent bulb is a very thin wire. The thin wire slows down electrical current. As a result, the thin wire heats up and glows. A fluorescent bulb uses a gas to produce light. Electric current makes the gas glow. Fluorescent bulbs are not as hot as incandescent bulbs.

Electric motors change electrical energy into motion. There are electric motors in toys, washing machines, tools, and even trains.

Electrical energy is useful, but it can be dangerous. When the protective covering on a wire rubs away, there can be a short circuit. The bare wire may touch a piece of metal or another wire. This "short circuit" can heat up the wire and cause a fire.

If you plug too many things in one outlet, too much current may go through a wire. Then the wire may get too hot and start a fire. Most homes have many outlets. These outlets are connected to different circuits. There is not too much current in any of these circuits.

Circuit breakers and fuses protect against dangerous amounts of electric current. A **circuit breaker** can stop the flow of charges. It can switch off a current that gets too high. A **fuse** breaks if the current gets too high. This causes an open circuit.

The hair dryer changes electrical energy into heat energy. ▼

◄ A circuit breaker breaks a circuit that has too much electric current. Then it can be reset and used again.

When the Lights Go Out

Blackouts remind us how electricity runs our lives.

Monica M. Davey/AFP/Getty Images

▲ **This blackout in California caused traffic problems. People used signs to help.**

W hen electricity goes out, there is a blackout. In a city, traffic lights do not work. Subways and elevators stop. Businesses lose money and time.

Lights Out in California

In January 2001, the lights went out in northern California. Traffic lights, bank machines, and classrooms lost electricity. First, one part of town had a blackout. An hour later, the lights went on. Then another part of town lost its electricity. Each area lost electricity for only one or two hours. However, there were traffic accidents. Businesses stopped working. Schools closed.

These rotating blackouts were planned by the Pacific Gas and Electric Company. California had not built any new power plants for many years. But now there was an enormous demand for electricity. There was not enough for everyone. So, people had to conserve electricity.

Thousands of New Yorkers walked over the Brooklyn Bridge during a blackout in 2003. ▼

Bklyn-Qns Expwy-Cadman Plaza W.
EXIT 3/4 MILE

Dan Herrick/Zuma/NewsCom

The Great Blackout of 1965

November 9, 1965 was a cold day. People in the northeastern part of the United States and Canada were using lots of electricity for heat and light. Then, in Toronto, Canada, at 5:15 p.m., an electrical relay failed. There was a surge of electricity. Local power lines shut down for safety, but the electricity had to go somewhere. It traveled down the power lines that connected Canada and the United States.

The lines filled with too much electricity. By 5:30, 80,000 square miles of the Northeast had a blackout, including Boston and New York City. However, by early the next morning, everyone's electricity returned. —*Lisa Jo Rudy*

AP Photo

Top Blackouts in the United States

April 15, 2003
A blackout affects **50 million** people in New York, NY; Albany, NY; Hartford, CT; Detroit, MI; Cleveland, OH; Toronto and Ontario; Canada.

July 13, 1977
9 million people in New York lose power.

November 9, 1965
25 million people lose electricity in Canada, New England, and New York.

▲ A blackout hits New York in 1965. People wait to use the telephone.

Description Writing Frame

Use the Writing Frame to orally summarize "Electricity."

All electricity is the result of _____.

Electric currents carry _____

_____.

Electrical objects change this energy into other kinds of energy,

such as _____.

For example, heat can be used _____

_____.

Electrical energy can also be changed into light, such as _____

_____.

Electric motors change electrical energy to motion. They are in many

things, **such as** _____

_____.

Electrical energy can be very useful.

Use the Writing Frame to write the summary on another sheet of paper. Be sure to include the **bold** signal words. Keep this as a model of this Text Structure.

Critical Thinking

1 Electrical charges can be _____.

    A. positive

    B. negative

    C. positive and negative

2 What is a rotating blackout? Find the paragraphs in "When the Lights Go Out" that explain it.

3 Find the sentences in "Electricity" that explain how charges affect each other.

4 Read the caption for the picture of California on page 20. Talk about this caption with a partner. What added information does it give that is not in the text?

> Photographs and captions give the reader additional information.

Digital Learning

For a list of links and activities that relate to this Science standard, visit the California Treasures Web site at www.macmillanmh.com to access the Content Reader resources.

Have students view the e-Review "Using Electrical Energy."

In addition, distribute copies of the Translated Concept Summaries in Spanish, Chinese, Hmong, Khmer, and Vietnamese.

Magnets

Magnets can make some objects move or even fly in the air! A magnet can affect an object without touching it.

When you put two magnets close together, they will repel or attract each other. Magnetic force is the force that pulls them together or pushes them apart. A **magnet** is any object with magnetic force.

Magnetic **poles** are the parts of a magnet where the magnetic force is strongest. All magnets have two poles. They have a north pole and a south pole. When two magnets come together, a north pole and a south pole attract each other. Like poles repel each other. Like poles are north-north and south-south.

The magnetic force between two magnets is weak when magnets are far apart. Magnetic force gets stronger when two magnets get closer. Then magnets can push or pull each other.

▼ Magnetic force pulls opposite poles together. It pushes like poles apart.

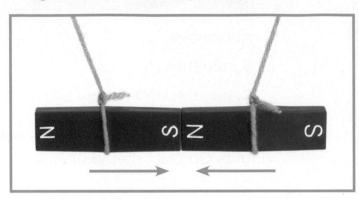

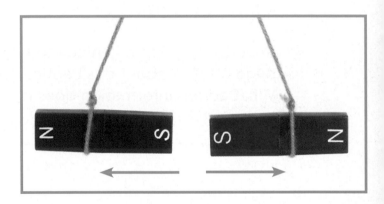

The aurora australis are lights in the sky near the South Pole. Charged particles from the Sun are caught in Earth's magnetic field. They give off light.

Every magnet has a magnetic field. A **magnetic field** is the area of magnetic force around a magnet. When one magnet enters the magnetic field of another magnet, it can be attracted or repelled. The magnets can do this without touching. Magnetic field is strongest near a magnet's poles.

Inside Earth there is a lot of melted iron. This iron sets up a magnetic field around Earth. Our planet is like a magnet.

Earth spins on its axis. Its axis is an imaginary line through the center of Earth. The geographic North Pole is at one end of this axis. The geographic South Pole is at the other end. Earth has one magnetic pole near its geographic North Pole and one near the geographic South Pole.

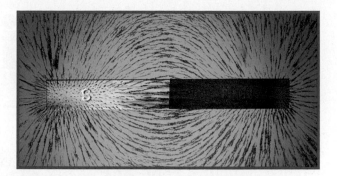

▲ Sprinkle iron filings around a bar magnet and they line up along the magnetic field. Magnetic field lines curve from one pole to another.

Long ago, people saw that one end of a magnet pointed north (to the north magnetic pole). People called this the north-seeking (or north) pole. The other end pointed south, so it was named the south-seeking (or south) pole.

Flying Trains!

A train that floats on air and has no wheels may sound like a dream of the future, but it's real, and it's here today.

AP Photo

▲ **A maglev train in Shanghai China carries people between the airport and the city 18 miles away.**

Some trains have no wheels. Maglev trains have magnets that levitate or raise the train above the ground. Maglev is short for "magnetic levitation." Because there is no rubbing on tracks and the trains have a special design, maglev trains move very fast.

Magnetic "Magic"

Maglev trains have large electromagnets under each car. An electromagnet works on an electric current. When the current runs through the wires, the electromagnet attracts and repels like an ordinary magnet. When the electric current is turned off, the electromagnet stops working.

Maglev trains run on special tracks. There are electrified coils of wire along the tracks. When the electricity is on, the coils of wire are magnetized. The magnets in the tracks repel the magnets in the trains. The power of the pushing magnets makes the trains float half an inch above the track.

Once the train floats, it needs to move. Electromagnets also help the train do this. The magnets in front of the train pull the train forward. The magnets behind the train push. The maglev train runs fast.

Maglev trains produce almost no pollution. They do not need much care and repair.

Future Maglev Trains

China and Japan were the first countries to use maglev trains day to day. England, Germany, and the United States may have maglev train service in the future. —*Lisa Jo Rudy*

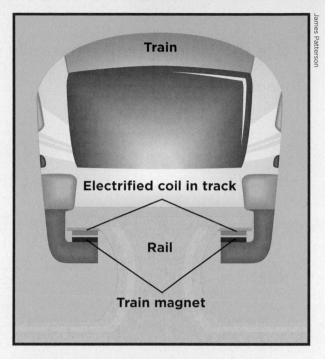

James Patterson

Train

Electrified coil in track

Rail

Train magnet

▲ **Electrified coils in the track repel magnets on the train. This causes the maglev train to lift up.**

Bernd Mellmann/Alamy

In Shanghai, China, a maglev train seems to fly over a road.

Sequence Writing Frame

Use the Writing Frame to orally summarize "Flying Trains!"

Maglev is short for _____

_____.

How do maglev trains work? **First**, they have _____

_____.

Next, trains run on _____

_____.

Then, the power of the magnets pushing against each other makes

_____

_____.

Finally, _____

_____.

Use the Writing Frame to write the summary on another sheet of paper. Be sure to include the **bold** signal words. Keep this as a model of this Text Structure.

Critical Thinking

1   A magnetic field is the area of _____ around a magnet.

    A. magnetic force

    B. magnetic poles

    C. magnetic particles

2   Maglev trains can move very fast. Reread the sentence in "Flying Trains!" that explains why.

3   Point out the paragraph in "Magnets" that explains how the north and south poles of magnets were named.

4   Find the picture on page 25 of the magnetic field of a bar magnet. Do you think the Earth's magnetic field looks the same or different? Discuss your ideas in a small group.

Photographs and captions give the reader additional information.

Digital Learning

For a list of links and activities that relate to this Science standard, visit the California Treasures Website at www.macmillanmh.com to access the Content Reader resources.

Have students view the e-Review "Magnets."

In addition, distribute copies of the Translated Concept Summaries in Spanish, Chinese, Hmong, Khmer, and Vietnamese.

Plants

Plants are living things. We use them for food. We use them to make clothes, too. Plants also produce a gas that we breathe. This gas is called oxygen. Plants help make life possible on Earth.

Plants can be different sizes and shapes. However, most plants are alike in one way. They make their own food. They use a process called **photosynthesis**.

All living things need energy. Energy helps them live, grow, and reproduce. Reproduce means to make more of one's own kind. Plants get the energy they need from the food they make.

During photosynthesis, plants take in sunlight, water, and a gas called carbon dioxide. Plants use these things to make food—sugar.

Photosynthesis

Plants take in sunlight.

Plants produce oxygen.

Plants take in carbon dioxide.

Plants take in water and nutrients from the soil.

Animals depend on plants for food energy.

Most plants need photosynthesis to live and grow. You need photosynthesis, too. Most animals depend on it because animals cannot make their own food. They must eat other living things to get the energy they need. Plants provide the energy that moves from one living thing to another.

Plants capture energy from the Sun to make their own food.

They use this food to grow and reproduce. They also store some food energy in their roots. When an animal, such as a grasshopper, eats a plant, stored energy passes from the plant to the animal. The animal uses most of this energy to grow and reproduce. It also stores some energy. When another animal, such as a bird, eats the grasshopper, stored energy passes to the bird.

Bad News for Bees

The latest buzz on honeybees is that they are disappearing and no one is sure why.

Where did all the bees go? Beekeepers, scientists, and farmers want to know why millions of honeybees are disappearing.

Twenty-four states have reported problems with bee colonies. A colony is a large group of bees that live and work together. These states (and maybe more) have lost bees. Honey production is down across the nation.

Busy Bees

Honeybees are insects that make honey. They also help flowering plants live and grow. First, bees move a powdery material called pollen from one part of a flower to another. This process is called pollination. Then a plant can grow seeds and fruit. Bees are important for crops, such as apples and almonds. Crops may be in trouble without enough bees.

HHS/The Plain Dealer/Landov

▲ A beekeeper examines a bee hive.

Honey Production in the United States

= states reporting bee loss

= states not reporting

Source: Bee Alert Technologies, Inc. And Lupin Logic. Inc

How Bees Work

Honeybees are some of nature's most important pollen carriers. First, honeybees crawl around a plant blossom. They collect sweet nectar from the blossom. The bees' legs get covered with pollen.

Then the bees fly to another blossom. Some of the pollen from the first blossom gets on the second blossom. Now a fruit or vegetable can grow.

Farms rent colonies of bees to carry pollen to their crops. Beekeepers take them in boxes from one farm to another. If honeybees do not carry pollen, many crops cannot produce fruit or seeds. Honeybees have a big job. They carry pollen to one third of the crops in the world!

A Big Problem to Solve

Experts met in Florida in February 2007. They worked to solve the mystery of the missing bees. Maybe a disease is killing the bees. Maybe the weather is too hot. No one knows. —*Andrea Delbanco*

Joe Raedle/Getty Images

▲ The bee will carry pollen from this blossom to another.

Jack Fields/Corbis

Bees are in the boxes. Farmers use the bees to pollinate their crops.

Problem/Solution Writing Frame

**Use the Writing Frame to orally summarize
"Bad News for Bees."**

Millions of honeybees are disappearing. **As a result**, honey

production _____

_____ .

Honeybees also help _____

_____

_____ .

If honeybees don't _____ , **then** _____

_____

_____ .

To solve the mystery of the missing bees _____

_____

_____ .

Use the Writing Frame to write the summary on another sheet
of paper. Be sure to include the **bold** signal words. Keep this as
a model of this Text Structure.

Critical Thinking

1 During photosynthesis a plant uses all of the following except
_____ .

    A. sugar

    B. sunlight

    C. carbon dioxide

2 Locate the paragraph in "Bad News for Bees" that explains how honeybees pollinate.

3 Find the sentences in "Plants" that explain the importance of plants.

4 Talk about the map on page 32 with a partner. What does the map tell you?

Maps are drawings of geographic locations such as a city, state, or park.

Digital Learning

For a list of links and activities that relate to this Science standard, visit the California Treasures Website at www.macmillanmh.com to access the Content Reader resources.

Have students view the e-Review "Plants and Sunlight."

In addition, distribute copies of the Translated Concept Summaries in Spanish, Chinese, Hmong, Khmer, and Vietnamese.

The Food Chain

Living things need energy to live and grow. They get energy from food. A **food chain** shows how energy passes from one living thing to another as food. First, a plant uses the Sun's energy to make its own food. Next, an animal, such as an insect, eats the plant. Then another animal, such as a bird, eats that insect. Energy passes from the Sun to the plant to the insect to the bird.

Green plants in a food chain are called **producers**. They make, or produce, their own food. Animals are called **consumers**. Animals cannot make their own food. They must eat, or consume, plants or other animals for food.

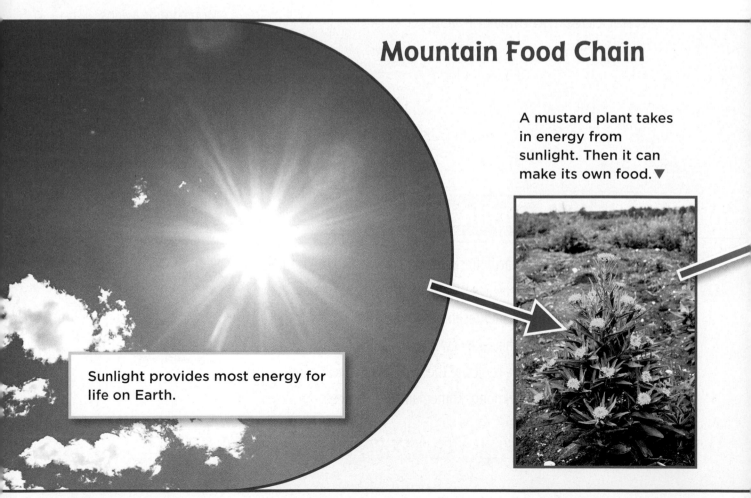

Mountain Food Chain

A mustard plant takes in energy from sunlight. Then it can make its own food. ▼

Sunlight provides most energy for life on Earth.

Herbivores are animals that eat mainly plants. They are called **primary consumers** because they are the first consumer in a food chain. Animals that eat other animals are called **carnivores**. Animals that eat plants and animals are called **omnivores**.

Sunlight begins nearly all food chains. A plant, or producer, is next in the chain. Then an animal eats the plant. Next, another animal eats the plant eater. The chain continues. Finally, tiny living things break down dead plants and animals. They return nutrients to the soil. These tiny living things are decomposers. The nutrients they return to the soil are used by new plants. Then the chain begins again.

Matter and energy pass from one living thing to another in a food chain. Only a small amount of energy passes from one living thing to another. This is because living things use a lot of energy from food to live and grow.

▲ A gopher eats the mustard plant.

A weasel eats the gopher. ▶

A mountain lion eats the weasel. ▶

▲ The mountain lion dies. Its body is broken down by decomposers.

Welcome Back, Grizzly Bears

Grizzly bears in Yellowstone National Park are off the endangered animals list, but they still need protection.

franzfoto.com / Alamy

G rizzly bears in Yellowstone National Park, in Wyoming, were put on the endangered animals list in 1975. This was because there were only about 300 bears in the park. Now there are more than 500 grizzly bears in Yellowstone. The bears are not endangered animals anymore. People worked hard to make this happen.

Grizzly bears are also called brown bears. They stand about 7 feet tall and weigh up to 600 pounds. These meat-eaters are at the top of the food chain. However, humans hunt grizzlies. Humans also build homes and businesses near where grizzlies live. This is difficult for the bears. The bears need a lot of space.

▲ A female grizzly and her cub are in Yellowstone National Park.

Time for Kids

▲ Yellowstone National Park is in Wyoming.

Help the Bears

Chris Servheen works for the U.S. Fish and Wildlife Service. He thinks it is important to prevent bears from dying. "Because fewer bears die, more bears live to have cubs," Servheen said. Officials closed roads to protect places where the bears live. They worked to help bears and visitors live together in the park.

Not all grizzly bears are safe. Four groups of grizzly bears in the United States are still on the endangered animals list.

Not all people think the Yellowstone bears are safe. More than 250 scientists and researchers sent a letter to the government. They want the Yellowstone grizzlies to be put back on the endangered animals list. However, Servheen says his organization has systems to help with the problems. —*Andrea Delbanco*

AP Photo

▲ **All grizzlies in the United States need protection.**

Erwin and Peggy Bauer/Animals Animals

Grizzlies Are Important

Grizzly bears live in the same places as black bears, wolves, deer, and elk. Grizzlies eat cutthroat trout, white bark pine nuts, and other animals and plants. When the grizzlies do well, other animals and plants that live in the same places do well, too.

Compare/Contrast Writing Frame

Use the Writing Frame to orally summarize "The Food Chain."

All living things need energy to live and grow.

Green plants are called _____.

Animals are called _____.

Both producers and consumers get energy from _____.

In some ways, however, _____

and _____ are **different**.

They are **different** because producers _____

_____.

Consumers are **different** from producers because _____

_____.

So _____ and _____
are **alike** and **different**.

Use the Writing Frame to write the summary on another sheet of paper. Be sure to include the **bold** signal words. Keep this as a model of this Text Structure.

Critical Thinking

1. Which type of organism makes its own food?

   A. producer

   B. decomposer

   C. consumer

2. Find the sentence in "Welcome Back, Grizzly Bears" that tells where grizzlies fit into the food chain.

3. Find the section in "The Food Chain" that tells the difference between herbivores, carnivores, and omnivores.

4. What does the inset map on page 38 show you?

> An inset map is a bigger picture of a small section of the map.

Digital Learning

For a list of links and activities that relate to this Science standard, visit the California Treasures Web site at www.macmillanmh.com to access the Content Readers resources.

Have students view the e-Review "Food Chains."

In addition, distribute copies of the Translated Concept Summaries in Spanish, Chinese, Hmong, Khmer, and Vietnamese.

Decomposers

Countless leaves fall to the forest floor each fall and winter. Some trees die. By the spring, there are fewer dead leaves on the ground. The dead trees start to rot.

What causes this cleanup? **Decomposers** do this job for an environment. Decomposers are consumers that break down dead plants and animals. They break them down into materials that plants can use again.

▲ The decomposers growing on this branch are called fungi. They slowly break down this branch.

▲ Most earthworms eat dead plant life. Earthworms pass nutrients from dead plants to the soil.

There are many types of decomposers. Earthworms break down plants. Plantlike organisms called **fungi** break down wood and other plant parts. Other decomposers break down dead animals. Decomposers work together.

The broken-down dead plants and animals may become part of the soil. This adds nutrients to soil that help plants grow well. Now the food chain starts all over again.

Some insects, such as this beetle, are decomposers. Flies and wasps are also insect decomposers. ▶

Food to Flowers

A California program shows kids how to recycle school lunch leftovers into food for plants.

California has many ideas on how to reduce, reuse, and recycle things. Your lunch leftovers can be healthful food for plants! A program in San Francisco, called *Food to Flowers!*, turns leftover school lunches into compost. Compost is a natural fertilizer for plants.

What Is Compost?

Compost is made in a natural process that breaks down organic matter. Organic matter is anything that was once alive.

Leaves, grass, paper (which comes from trees), and most types of food can be made into compost. The organic material is mixed together. Decomposers such as insects, worms, and fungi start to break it down. They live in the organic material.

Over time, decomposers turn organic matter into a dark, crumbly material that looks like soil. It helps plants grow.

Phoebe the Phoenix, the *Food to Flowers!* mascot ▶

Les Gibbon/Alamy

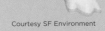

Courtesy SF Environment

How *Food to Flowers!* Works

Food to Flowers! puts big green carts in school lunchrooms. Kids put in their leftover food scraps and dirty paper products after lunch. Then, a local waste hauler takes the carts to a composting facility. People grind the leftovers into very small pieces and make them into compost. It is used for farms and gardens.

Composting turns leftover food and paper products into something useful.

Other Great Ideas for the Environment

Another program, called *Waste-Free Lunch,* was created for every kid in every school. You do not use as many plastics and other non-recyclable materials when you pack a waste-free lunch. —*Lisa Jo Rudy*

Courtesy SF Environment

▲ Kids dump their lunch leftovers into a *Food to Flowers!* cart.

How to Pack a Waste-Free Lunch

Do Include

- Sandwiches and snacks in reusable containers
- Whole fruits without packages
- Drinks in reusable thermoses or recyclable cans
- Reusable cloth napkin and utensils

Do Not Include

- Individually wrapped snacks
- Disposable forks and spoons and plastic bags

Sequence Writing Frame

Use the Writing Frame to orally summarize "Food to Flowers."

A California program called *Food to Flowers!* turns leftover school lunches into compost. Compost is made in a natural

process that _____

_____ .

First, *Food to Flowers!* puts _____

_____ .

After lunch, _____

_____ .

Next, _____

_____ .

Then, people _____

_____ .

Finally, the compost is used for _____

_____ .

Use the Writing Frame to write the summary on another sheet of paper. Keep this as a model of this Text Structure.

Critical Thinking

1 Fungi break down _____.

    A. only plants

    B. animals

    C. wood and other plant parts

2 Find the sentences in "Food to Flowers" that describe organic matter.

3 Point to the word on page 42 that defines what breaks down plants and animals that are dead.

4 With a partner, orally create your own caption for the photo on page 45.

Photographs and captions give visual examples that help explain the text.

Digital Learning

For a list of links and activities that relate to this Science standard, visit the California Treasures Web site at www.macmillanmh.com to access the Content Readers resources.

Have students view the Science in Motion "Microorganisms at Work." In addition, distribute copies of the Translated Concept Summaries in Spanish, Chinese, Hmong, Khmer, and Vietnamese.

Ecosystems

Most plants live in soil. Birds may use grasses to make nests. Bacteria in the soil break down leaves. Living and nonliving things interact, or have an effect on one another, every day. An **ecosystem** is all the interacting parts of an environment. An ecosystem can be large, such as a redwood forest. It can also be small, such as a pond.

All ecosystems are made up of living and nonliving things. The living things that shape an ecosystem are called **biotic factors**.

The nonliving things that shape an ecosystem are called **abiotic factors**. Temperature, rain, snow, ice, sunlight, and soil are abiotic factors.

Pond Ecosystem

1. Many plants live on the water's edge. They get water and nutrients from the soil.

2. Birds use pond plants to make nests.

3. Frogs feast on insects they find around the pond.

4. Turtles come to the water's surface to get air. They get warmth from the Sun, too.

Ponds, deserts, rain forests and coral reefs are examples of ecosystems. Each has its own living things, soil, and climate. Climate describes the typical weather patterns of an area over time.

The biotic and abiotic factors of an ecosystem work together. For example, plants in a pond need a lot of water. They also need a certain kind of soil to grow well. Pond animals need a special climate.

Stop the Spartina!

Spartina is a helpful plant when it grows in the right place. However, in the Puget Sound in Washington State, spartina is a terrible weed.

Scientists call plants and animals that start growing in the wrong place aliens or exotics. Spartina, or cordgrass, is native to many East Coast waters. But in Washington, spartina is an alien plant.

An Alien Attacks

Spartina spreads easily. It has pushed out native plants in many parts of Puget Sound. Also, spartina grows in thick clumps. These clumps change the mudflats around the sound. First, native plants and the slopes of the mudflats disappear. Then, native animals, such as crabs, snails, salmon, and shorebirds have less to eat. So they leave the area.

Students at Lincoln Elementary School in Mount Vernon, Washington decided to solve the spartina problem. First, they did some research.

Jack Thomas

▲ **These students wanted to solve the spartina problem.**

Galen Rowell/Mountain Light/Alamy

▲ **Spartina grows in thick clumps. This harms the mudflats.**

Where Did It Come From?

First, settlers from the East came to the West in the 1800s to raise oysters. They brought the oysters packed in wet spartina. When they put the oysters in Puget Sound, the spartina seeds sprouted.

Spartina was also introduced to the area on purpose. Duck hunters planted it to attract more ducks. Engineers used it to help keep soil from being washed or blown away. Farmers planted it to feed their cattle.

Take Action

It will take hard work, money, and time to get rid of spartina. The Lincoln Elementary students educated the public and the government. They held town meetings. They also traveled to the state capital in Olympia to talk about the problem. They went to a bay in Puget Sound to cut off spartina seed heads. This kept the weed from spreading. However, it will take many years to solve the spartina problem completely. —*David Bjerklie*

▼ **Spartina harms Puget Sound.**

Terry Donnelly

Description Writing Frame

Use the Writing Frame to orally summarize "Ecosystems."

Ecosystems have many interesting **characteristics**. An ecosystem is

_____

_____ .

An ecosystem is made up of _____

_____ .

Biotic factors are _____

_____ .

Another characteristic that shapes an ecosystem is _____

_____ .

Because of these characteristics, there are many kinds of ecosystems.

Use the Writing Frame to write the summary on another sheet of paper. Be sure to include the **bold** signal words. Keep this as a model of this Text Structure.

Critical Thinking

1 Plants, animals and microorganisms are _____.

  A. abiotic factors

  B. biotic factors

  C. critical factors

2 Find the sentence in "Stop the Spartina!" that explains what alien plants are. Discuss with a partner.

3 Point to the place in "Ecosystems" that explains the role of climate in an ecosystem. Discuss with a partner.

4 Look at the diagram on pages 48–49. Read the numbered captions. How do the living and nonliving things in the pond interact?

Captions help explain the diagram.

Digital Learning

For a list of links and activities that relate to this Science standard, visit the California Treasures Web site at www.macmillanmh.com to access the Content Readers resources.

Have students view the e-Review "Ecosystems."

In addition, distribute copies of the Translated Concept Summaries in Spanish, Chinese, Hmong, Khmer, and Vietnamese.

Ecosystems Change

Ecosystems are always changing. Over time they can become warmer or colder, wetter or drier. Over millions of years mountain ranges can be built up or broken down. Lakes can dry up or fill in. Living things may not be able to survive.

Some living things can survive changes by changing how they live. An **accommodation** is an individual living thing's response to change. For example, the food supply of some animals may be destroyed by a fire. Some animals will change what they eat to survive. They may also be less active to survive with less food. Some animals will use other plants or materials as shelter.

Not all animals can change as an ecosystem changes. Food and clean water may be hard to find after a fire. Some animals must find a new place to live. They must look for food, water, and shelter there.

Some changes can help an ecosystem. A fire can keep an ecosystem from becoming too crowded. Overcrowding, or too many plants and animals, can keep them from getting what they need.

▼ A fire can change a forest ecosystem quickly. Some living things can survive these changes.

Some living things do not move after an ecosystem changes. They may slowly die out. An animal or plant that has very few left of its kind is **endangered**. Some endangered plants and animals become **extinct**. This means there are no more of their kind.

When an ecosystem changes, many animals have adaptations to survive. Adaptations are special body parts or ways of doing things. They help living things survive in their environment. A fish's gills and an eagle's sharp eyes are adaptations. Adaptations can help animals move, catch food, and live in certain climates.

Adaptations can help living things protect themselves. For example, some animals are not seen because they blend into their environment. This adaptation is called **camouflage**. Some animals are not seen because they look like other living things. This adaptation is called **mimicry**.

How do adaptations come about? Think of a giraffe's long neck. This trait, or characteristic, was passed down from one generation to the next. Long ago, many giraffes' necks were shorter. The tallest giraffes could reach leaves in trees to get more food. These giraffes survived. Over time, giraffes with shorter necks died out. The study of how organisms pass traits from one generation to the next is called **genetics**.

▲ There is an Indian leaf butterfly in this picture. Mimicry helps it hide.

▲ A giraffe's long neck helps it to reach leaves. It helps it see predators.

A Very Hairy Crab

Scientists discover an unknown crab off the coast of Easter Island.

Crabs can be red, blue, brown, and green. Now, scientists have discovered an unknown kind of crab. This crab is covered with blonde hair.

In 2006, scientists announced they had found this new crab. A team from the United States and France caught the crab near Easter Island in the Pacific Ocean. The crab was 7,540 feet down.

The crab has a scientific name. It is *Kiwa hirsuta*. *Kiwa* is the name of the Polynesian goddess of shellfish, too. *Hirsuta* means "hairy." Scientists also gave the crab a nickname: Yeti.

"This is a very rare find," said Joe Jones, one of the scientists.

A New Family

Kiwa hirsuta is about six inches long. Its body has no color. Its hair covers its pincers. Some other crabs have similar hair. This unknown kind of crab is not alone. Scientists say that it is part of a group, or family, of different kinds of crabs that was not known before.

▼ The *Kiwa hirsuta* is covered with hair. The hair covers the crab's pincers.

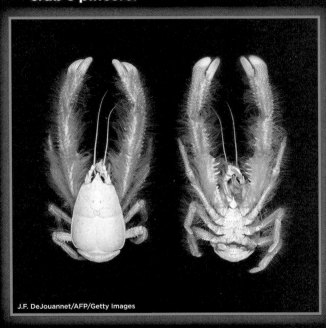

J.F. DeJouannet/AFP/Getty Images

▼ The new crab was found near other crustaceans.

Ralph White/Corbis

MBari/B. Vrijenhoek/Newscom

Michel Segonzac is a scientist at the French Research Institute for Exploitation of the Sea. He helped discover the crab. He says that the "hair" around the pincers contains lots of bacteria. The bacteria may filter out poisons in the water. The bacteria help the crab to survive.

▲ The hairy crab has "hairy" legs. The "hair" has lots of bacteria.

Kiwa hirsuta is blind. Many deep-sea creatures do not need to see because there is no light down there.

Deep Ocean Vents

The hairy crab lives in a strange world. There is almost no life on the deep ocean floor. Light cannot go past the first 300 feet of ocean water. Algae are tiny plantlike living things. Most algae cannot live below that. Without algae, there is no food chain of fish and other animals.

In some places there are deep ocean vents, or holes. These vents are called hydrothermal vents. They release gases and hot water. Volcanoes make this deep water hot. The heat is energy for these places.

Ralph White/Corbis

▲ Giant tubeworms live near hydrothermal vents.

Some strange creatures are able to use this heat energy. Giant tubeworms and huge clams live near deep ocean vents in the Pacific Ocean. Eyeless shrimp live near these vents in the Atlantic Ocean. Now the hairy crab is one of the animals that can survive in this special environment. —*Richie Chevat*

Cause/Effect Writing Frame

**Use the Writing Frame to orally summarize
"A Very Hairy Crab."**

The *Kiwa hirsuta* lives deep in the Pacific Ocean. There is almost

no light that deep in the ocean. **As a result**, _____

_____ .

Kiwa hirsuta is about _____

long. Its body has _____

The _____

_____

contain bacteria. **Because of this** _____

_____ .

Hydrothermal vents provide energy for deep in the ocean.

This explains why _____

_____ .

Use the Writing Frame to write the summary on another sheet
of paper. Be sure to include the **bold** signal words. Keep this as a
model of this Text Structure.

Critical Thinking

1   An individual organism's response to a change in the
    ecosystem is called _____.

> **A.** accommodation
>
> **B.** endangered
>
> **C.** genetics

2   Locate text in "A Very Hairy Crab" that explains what *Kiwa
    hirsuta* means. Discuss with a partner.

3   Point to the definition of mimicry in "Ecosystems Change."

4   Look at the pictures on the bottom of page 54.
    With a partner, describe how the pictures show
    how an ecosystem can change.

> Photographs provide
> visual examples of facts
> that appear in a text.

Digital Learning

For a list of links and activities that relate to this Science standard,
visit the California Treasures Web site at www.macmillanmh.com to
access the Content Readers resources.

Have students view the e-Review, **"Changes in Ecosystems."**

In addition, distribute copies of the Translated Concept Summaries in
Spanish, Chinese, Hmong, Khmer, and Vietnamese.

Pollination and Seed Dispersal

Flowers depend on animals in many ways. Flowering plants reproduce when male cells are transported, or moved, to female cells. This process is called **pollination**.

Animals such as bees, hummingbirds, butterflies, and bats help with pollination. They travel from flower to flower. They collect a sweet drink inside the flower called **nectar**. A powdery material called **pollen** rubs off the stamen of the flower and onto the animal's body. The pollen has male cells.

Then the animal visits other flowers. Then some of this pollen rubs off on the pistil of the flowers. Then the flowers can make seeds. When seeds are planted, a plant can grow.

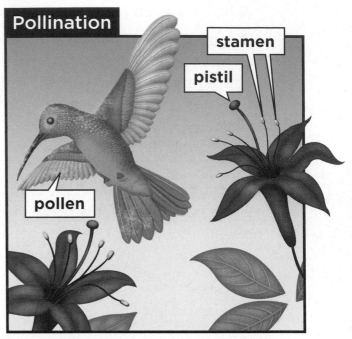

Pollination

stamen

pistil

pollen

A bee lands on a flower. Pollen rubs onto its body.

▲ This iguana eats a punta cactus fruit. The fruit seeds are dispersed in the animal's waste.

In time, a fruit forms from a part of the flower. Seeds are stored inside the fruit.

How do the seeds inside fruit get planted in the ground? **Seed dispersal** is the process of spreading seeds. In this process, seeds are left in a place where they can grow into new plants. Animals are an important part of seed dispersal.

First, an animal eats a fruit and its seeds. Then the seeds are left on the ground in the animal's waste. The seeds may grow into a new plant.

Some plants have sticky seeds. These seeds can stick to an animal's fur. When the animal moves to a new place, the seeds rub off. They fall to the ground. They may grow into new plants there.

Bats!

You may think bats do not have a great reputation, but they are very helpful.

Some people think bats are harmful. However, most bats, including California's brown bat and the Mexican long-tongued bat, are harmless. Bats do not drink human blood! They eat insects and fruit. Also, California's bats help the ecosystem.

Bats and Plants

Mexican long-tongued bats do have very long tongues. These tongues help them eat nectar and pollen deep down inside agaves and cactus flowers. When bats fly from flower to flower, they carry pollen. Bats carry pollen that helps plants in California's deserts reproduce.

Bats that eat fruit are very important in the tropics. Major crops, such as bananas, dates, figs, and vanilla depend on bats for pollination. Farmers need bats. Bats help them grow more crops to sell.

A little brown bat eats an insect. ▶

Bats and Bugs

Adult little brown bats are only four inches tall. They eat an incredible number of bugs. Their favorite foods are insects that bite, such as mosquitoes. One little brown bat can eat 600 mosquitoes in one hour! Mosquitoes can cause serious diseases. Little brown bats help keep mosquitoes in check. —*Lisa Jo Rudy*

Joe McDonald/Animals Animals

Facts About Bats

It is not always easy to find bats. Here are some ways to help you.

- Look for bats at sunrise or sunset.

- Look for a place where you can see bats' dark wings against a lighter sky.

- Look in areas where there are a lot of bugs flying at night. Look near water.

- Look near lights outside. Bats eat insects that go near lights.

Bats are important to the ecosystem. Do not disturb bats that are asleep or hibernating.

Bats go out at night to hunt insects.

Merlin D. Tuttle, Bat Conservation International

Compare/Contrast Writing Frame

Use the Writing Frame to orally summarize "Pollination and Seed Dispersal."

The processes of pollination and seed dispersal are **similar**

because they help plants _____ .

In pollination _____

_____ .

Unlike pollination, _____

is the process of spreading seeds. It is **different** from pollination

because _____ .

Seed dispersal and pollination are the **same** in that _____

and _____ both can stick to _____ .

However, in seed dispersal the **difference** is that the seeds _____

_____ .

Here they may grow into new plants.

Use the Writing Frame to write the summary on another sheet of paper. Be sure to include the **bold** signal words. Keep this as a model of this Text Structure.

Critical Thinking

1 The sweet drink inside flowers is called _____.

    A. seeds

    B. dispersal

    C. nectar

2 Locate the text in "Bats!" that explains how bats help plants. Discuss with a partner.

3 Find the section in "Bats!" that tells you how to find bats.

4 Look at the diagram on page 60. Discuss with a partner how the bird helps with pollination.

Diagrams usually contain labels that help identify each part.

Digital Learning

For a list of links and activities that relate to this Science standard, visit the California Treasures Web site at www.macmillanmh.com to access the Content Readers resources.

Have students view the Science in Motion "Pollination."

In addition, distribute copies of the Translated Concept Summaries in Spanish, Chinese, Hmong, Khmer, and Vietnamese.

Plants for Food and Shelter

Animals depend on plants. Animals breathe the oxygen that plants produce. They depend on plants for food. They also use plants for shelter and protection.

Every part of a plant is food for some animal. Caterpillars and rabbits eat plant leaves. Other animals, such as beetles, eat plant roots and stems. Animals such as earthworms and snails eat plants that are dead. Bears, birds, bats, monkeys, and lizards eat fruits and seeds.

Even meat-eaters depend on plants for food. Remember, plants take in the Sun's energy and use it to make food from raw material around them. Some animals get this food directly by eating plants. Plant-eaters, in turn, can be food for meat-eaters. Directly or indirectly, all animals need plants for food.

▲ Squirrels use nuts for energy.

Animals make nests and other shelters from plants. Squirrels move into tree holes. They make a bed of soft moss and leaves. Many birds collect twigs and sticks and weave them into a nest. Birds use the nests to keep their eggs and babies safe.

An animal senses danger. What does it do? Hide! Leafhoppers and garter snakes hide in the grass for shelter and safety. Rabbits or birds hide in the bushes. Fish hide in thick seaweed in the ocean. Plants help keep animals safe.

▲ The grass allows the snake to hide from predators. The color of the snake and the grass are the same.

The bird uses twigs and plant materials to build its nest. Nests provide a safe place where birds can feed their young.

Are They Cousins?

Leopards once thought to be related turn out to be from completely different kinds of animals.

louded leopards are medium-sized wildcats. Their name comes from the cloudlike spots that help them hide in the jungle. They live on mainland Southeast Asia and the islands of Borneo and Sumatra. It was difficult to know about clouded leopards. This is because they live alone and tend to hide. Now we know more.

For more than 100 years, scientists believed that the clouded leopards in Southeast Asia and on Borneo and Sumatra were the same kind of animal. Researchers compared them very carefully. They found that the two leopards are two different animals.

▼ **This clouded leopard lives on the islands of Sumatra and Borneo.**

▼ **This clouded leopard lives on the mainland. It is a different animal from the clouded leopards that live on the islands.**

WWF-Canon/Alain Compost

Peter Weimann/Animals Animals

A Jungle Home

Many unique animals and plants live in the forests of Sumatra and Borneo. The governments of the three countries on Borneo agreed to protect this habitat. This will help the clouded leopard survive.

A Meat-Eater Needs Plants

Clouded leopards do not eat plants. However, the leopards do need plants to survive.

All food chains start when plants use sunlight to make food. Some animals are plant-eaters. They get energy by eating plants. These animals become food for meat-eaters, such as the clouded leopard.

The clouded leopard is part of many food chains. It eats many animals—monkeys, squirrels, and so on. All the food chains in an area are linked together into a food web. Food webs trace the flow of energy from the Sun to plants, to plant eaters, to meat eaters, and to animals that eat plants and animals.

Wayne Lawler/Corbis

▲ **The countries on Borneo agreed to protect the natural environment.**

Sequence Writing Frame

**Use the Writing Frame to orally summarize
"Are They Cousins?"**

Every plant and animal in the forest of Sumatra and Borneo is a part of the food web.

It **starts** with the _____ .

Plants use the _____

_____ .

Next, plant-eaters get _____ by _____ .

Then the clouded leopard and other meat-eaters _____

_____ .

That is how energy passes on _____

_____ .

This flow of energy is what keeps a food web going.

Use the Writing Frame to write the summary on another sheet of paper. Be sure to include the **bold** signal words. Keep this as a model of this Text Structure.

Critical Thinking

1 Many animals depend on plants for shelter and _____.

    A. pollination

    B. seed dispersal

    C. food

2 Point to the place in the text "Plants for Food and Shelter" that mentions how animals depend on plants for shelter. Discuss with a partner.

3 Find the sentence in "Are They Cousins?" that describes how the clouded leopard's body helps it survive in the jungle.

4 Look at the globe on page 68. Why is it important to the article "Are They Cousins?"

A globe helps you find the place you are reading about.

Digital Learning

For a list of links and activities that relate to this Science standard, visit the California Treasures Web site at www.macmillanmh.com to access the Content Readers resources.

Have students view the e-Review "Living Things Need Each Other." In addition, distribute copies of the Translated Concept Summaries in Spanish, Chinese, Hmong, Khmer, and Vietnamese.

Microorganisms

You cannot see them, but there are tiny living things everywhere. They are on the food you eat. They are on the book you are holding now. They are inside and outside your body. You can find them in oceans, lakes, ponds, and rivers. You can even find them in puddles.

What are these tiny creatures? They are microorganisms. **Microorganisms** are living things too small to be seen with just our eyes. Many microorganisms are made of only one cell. **Cells** are the smallest units of life. Plants and animals are made of many cells.

You can see most microorganisms through a tool called a microscope. A microscope shows a large view of an object. Many classroom microscopes magnify objects 30 to 60 times their actual size.

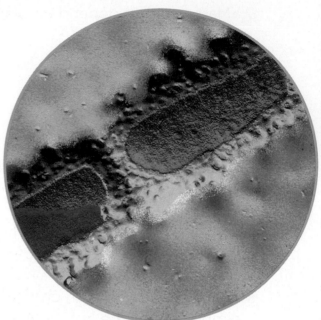

▲ Escherichia coli

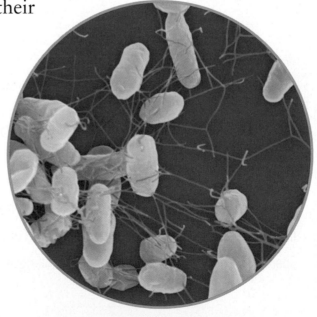

▲ Salmonella

There are many kinds of microorganisms. One of the smallest is called **bacteria**. Bacteria can be helpful or harmful to humans. Harmful bacteria cause illness. Helpful bacteria help humans swallow and digest food. They can even help fight disease.

Protists are another group of microorganisms. Many live in ponds and lakes. Protists can be helpful or harmful. Some protists eat bacteria. This keeps harmful bacteria under control. Other protists cause disease.

How do protists compare to bacteria? They are much larger than bacteria. They have parts that make and use food. They even have parts that make new protists.

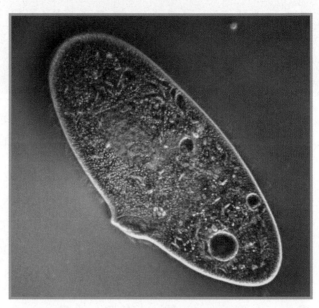

▲ This is what a protist looks like under a microscope.

You Can Prevent Disease

We can keep harmful microorganisms out of our bodies. This table shows how people can stay healthy from diseases caused by microorganisms.

Disease	Microorganism	Prevention
tooth decay	tooth bacteria	Brush and floss your teeth.
Lyme disease	bacteria in ticks	Wear long pants on hikes.
dysentery	amoeba-like protist	Drink clean water.
malaria	protist in mosquitoes	Use anti-malaria medicine.
food poisoning	salmonella bacteria	Cook and touch food properly.

"GOOD GERMS"

Some germs have a bad reputation they don't deserve.

You wash your hands to get rid of germs. This is a good idea. However, not all germs are harmful.

When we say *germ*, we are talking about bacteria—or smaller particles called viruses. Bacteria can cause terrible diseases. They can also be helpful. You have hundreds of different kinds of bacteria in your body. They help you break down the food you eat into nutrients you can use.

Good Germs Fight Bad Germs

Doctors use medicines called antibiotics to kill harmful bacteria. On the other hand, antibiotics can cause diarrhea and stomach problems. Nutritionists say that helpful germs called probiotics can help you handle antibiotics. Probiotics can help you fight diarrhea, too.

Helpful germs can even help you fight some diseases. Probiotics can make the body's defenses stronger. You can fight harmful germs off more easily with extra probiotics.

This is a good germ under a microscope. ▶

This girl takes medicine for strep throat. Probiotics help her stomach feel good.

Germs Made for Kids

Kids get a lot of bacterial infections, such as earaches and strep throat. Doctors give kids antibiotics to treat those infections. Many times, kids get diarrhea and other stomach problems from antibiotics. Probiotics can help kids feel better when they take antibiotics.

Eat Your Germs!

Probiotics come in pills. Probiotics are also in delicious food, such as yogurt, buttermilk, and other milk products. —*Lisa Jo Rudy*

Yogurt has probiotics, or helpful germs. ▶

Compare/Contrast Writing Frame

Use the Writing Frame to orally summarize "Microorganisms."

Bacteria and protists are **both** _____.

They are **alike** because they are **both** _____

_____.

Helpful bacteria can _____

_____.

Harmful bacteria can _____.

Protists **differ** from bacteria in many ways.

One difference is that protists are _____

_____.

Another difference is that protists _____

_____.

Protists are also **different** because they have _____

_____.

Use the Writing Frame to write the summary on another sheet of paper. Be sure to include the **bold** signal words. Keep this as a model of this Text Structure.

Critical Thinking

1 Microorganisms that are larger than bacteria are called
_____ .

    A. protists

    B. producers

    C. harmful

2 What helpful and harmful effects can antibiotics have? Find the section in "Good Germs" that gives the answer. Discuss it with a partner.

3 Show a partner the sentences in "Good Germs" that describe how probiotics are helpful.

4 Discuss the table on page 73 with a partner.

A table has columns and rows. Sometimes you read down the columns. Other times you read across rows.

Digital Learning

For a list of links and activities that relate to this Science standard, visit the California Treasures Web site at www.macmillanmh.com to access the Content Readers resources.

Have students view the e-Review "Microorganisms."

In addition, distribute copies of the Translated Concept Summaries in Spanish, Chinese, Hmong, Khmer, and Vietnamese.

Minerals and Rocks

Minerals are natural, nonliving substances in rocks. You can identify minerals by their properties. Properties include color, luster, streak, cleavage, and hardness.

Luster describes the way light reflects off the surface of a mineral. Some minerals are metallic, or shiny. Some minerals are dull. Others may be glassy.

Cleavage is the way a mineral splits or breaks. Some minerals, like mica, split into a thin sheet. Other minerals, like quartz, split unevenly.

Streak is the color of the powder left when you scratch a mineral along a white tile. This tile is called a streak plate. The streak of some minerals is the same color as the mineral. Other minerals have a streak that is a different color from the minerals.

Hardness is a mineral's ability to scratch another mineral or be scratched by another mineral. **Mohs' Hardness Scale** shows the hardness of some common minerals. Diamond is a 10 on the scale. It is the hardest mineral. Talc is a 1 on the scale. It is the softest mineral. There are many more minerals for each level of hardness.

Minerals with a lower number can be scratched by minerals with a higher number. ▶

▲ Pyrite, or fool's gold, has a metallic luster.

▲ Hematite leaves a red streak. You can see it on this streak plate.

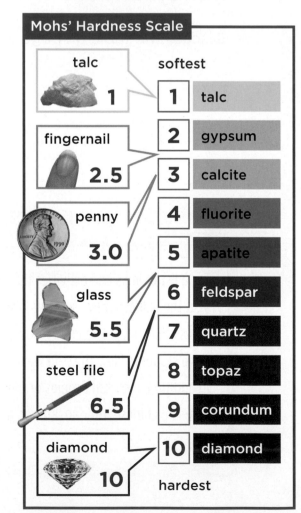

Mohs' Hardness Scale

talc **1**	softest
	1 talc
fingernail **2.5**	**2** gypsum
	3 calcite
penny **3.0**	**4** fluorite
	5 apatite
glass **5.5**	**6** feldspar
	7 quartz
steel file **6.5**	**8** topaz
	9 corundum
diamond **10**	**10** diamond
	hardest

Different processes on Earth form different kinds of rocks. Igneous rocks form when melted rock cools and hardens above or below the ground. The word *igneous* means "made by fire."

Tiny particles called **sediments** can form other rocks. Some sediments are tiny bits of rocks and minerals. Other sediments are bits of plants, bones, shells, or other animal materials. These sediments can settle into layers. Over time the layers change into sedimentary rock.

Extreme heat and pressure can change any rock into metamorphic rock. Over time, all rocks change from one kind to another. The **rock cycle** describes how rocks change from one kind to another.

The Rock Cycle

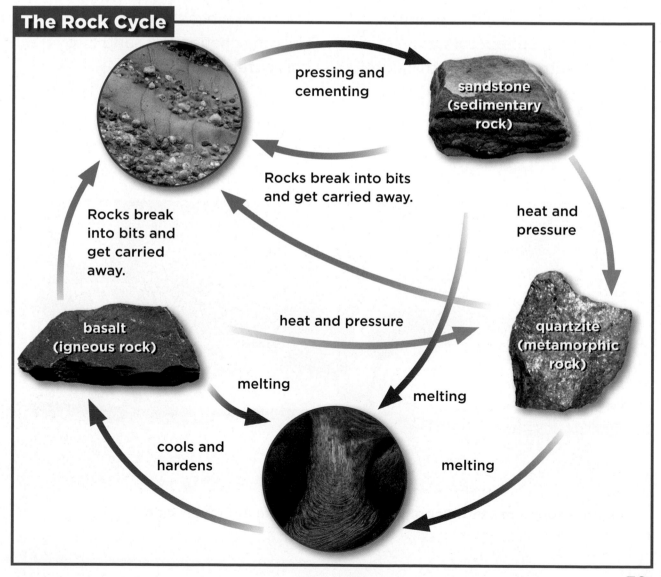

pressing and cementing

sandstone (sedimentary rock)

Rocks break into bits and get carried away.

Rocks break into bits and get carried away.

heat and pressure

basalt (igneous rock)

heat and pressure

quartzite (metamorphic rock)

melting

melting

cools and hardens

melting

Sand Helps Make Computers

Silicon is a substance found in sand. It is also the most important part of computer chips. Silicon is a semiconductor. Semiconductors are the best materials for making computer chips. Semiconductors only let a little electricity to pass through. This is perfect for the switches inside computer chips.

Silicon is very easy to find. Most sand starts out as rock. Then wind, water, and other rocks cause erosion. Huge rocks break down into smaller pieces over time. Then the small pieces become sand. Humans change the sand into computer chips.

Jupiter Images/Goodshot/Alamy

Silicon is found in sand. People use silicon to make computer chips.

We Make Computer Chips

People make computer chips with a scoop of sand. They heat the sand in a furnace. This produces pure silicon. Then they change the silicon into long, wide rods, or sticks. They are cut into thin wafers, or slices.

Meanwhile, engineers design the computer's circuits. Circuits are paths where electricity flows. They have switches that turn the electricity on and off. Engineers design these circuits on enormous pieces of paper.

Then the engineers shrink their designs to half-inch squares. Then they etch, or draw, the circuit designs onto the silicon wafers. They put metal over the circuits they etched. Then they put another silicon wafer on top. They etch another circuit design onto that silicon wafer. They add more metal circuits to the top of this silicon-and-circuit sandwich.

Engineers use a laser beam to cut their silicon-and-circuit sandwich into tiny computer chips. These computer chips may be used for office work, games, or making music. —*Lisa Jo Rudy*

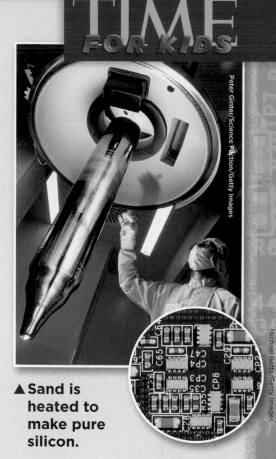

Peter Ginter/Science Faction/Getty Images

Michael Betts/Getty Images

▲ **Sand is heated to make pure silicon.**

▲ **This is a computer circuit.**

▼ **These people use objects that have silicon chips.**

Erin Patrice O'Brien/Getty Images

This is a silicon chip. ▶

John Foxx/Getty Images

Sequence Writing Frame

Use the Writing Frame to orally summarize "Sand Helps Make Computers."

Computer chips **start** with _____.

This sand is _____.

After that, the pure silicon is _____.

Meanwhile the engineers _____.

Next, they etch _____

_____.

Then they put _____

_____.

After that, they add metal circuits to the top of the silicon-and-circuit sandwich.

Finally, engineers use a laser beam to _____

_____.

These computer chips may be used for office work, games, or making music.

Use the frame to write the summary on another sheet of paper. Be sure to include the **bold** signal words. Keep this as a model of this Text Structure.

Critical Thinking

1 The way a mineral splits or breaks is called _____.

   A. streak

   B. cleavage

   C. hardness

2 Is silicon easy to find? Point to the sentence in "Sand Helps Make Computers" that answers this question.

3 Show a partner the sentence on page 79 that defines the rock cycle.

4 Review Mohs' Hardness Scale on page 78. Can a fingernail scratch glass? Discuss the scale with a partner.

Charts present information in a simple and organized way.

Digital Learning

For a list of links and activities that relate to this Science standard, visit the California Treasures Web site at www.macmillanmh.com to access the Content Readers resources.

Have students view the e-Review "Minerals: The Building Blocks of Rocks."

In addition, distribute copies of the Translated Concept Summaries in Spanish, Chinese, Hmong, Khmer, and Vietnamese.

Landforms Can Change

Landforms are natural features on Earth's surface. Some landforms change in just a short time. A mudslide can quickly change a hillside. Most landforms, however, change over a long time.

Water, waves, wind, and ice can change the shape of landforms. For example, rain flows downhill from the tops of mountains to the sea. The water forms a channel. It flows into streams and rivers. These rivers move downhill and cut away land. They carry away sediments. This process forms a **valley**.

▲ The waves erode this cliff in Cabo San Lucas, Mexico.

Running water changes the land on the sides and bottoms of streams and rivers. As it flows, a river carries sediment for miles. Then the river may flow into an ocean. The river slows down when it flows into the ocean. It drops off the sediments into the mouth, the end, of the river. These sediments form an area of land called a **delta**.

Waves can change a beach. Waves can break big parts of rock from the bottom of cliffs. This slowly makes the cliffs smaller. Waves can also pick up tons of sand. They can drop off the sand somewhere else. The size of a beach may shrink in one place. It may grow in another place. Powerful winds can cause large waves. The waves can wash away much of a beach in a few hours.

Wind Changes Land

Wind carries sand and bits of rock. It scratches the surface of rocks. This causes small bits of rock to break off. Then the wind carries them away. This type of erosion takes many years. Wind can also blow sand into hills called **sand dunes**. Sand dunes form when wind deposits particles of sand. Objects such as rocks or grasses block the wind. This slows the movement of the sand particles. Then a sand dune forms.

The colder parts of Earth have **glaciers**. Glaciers are large, thick sheets of ice that move slowly. Glaciers covered much of Earth millions of years ago.

Glaciers form in cold areas where more snow falls than melts. The thick snow slowly changes into ice. The bottom of the glacier melts a little. The glacier begins to flow downhill. Then ice at the bottom and sides of a glacier freezes onto rocks. The glacier continues to move. It tears the rocks out of the ground. The glacier tears rocks from the sides of a valley, too. Sometimes it moves enormous rocks. A glacier widens and deepens a valley, giving it a U shape.

A glacier forms a U-shaped valley. This valley is in White River National Forest, Colorado.

Alaska Has a Problem

Vincent J. Musi/Aurora

What's happening to an Alaska village may hold lessons for much bigger cities.

Shishmaref is a tiny village in Alaska. It has a problem. Global warming is hurting Shishmaref. Warmer temperatures cause ice to melt. Ocean levels are starting to rise. The village has lost between 100 and 300 feet of coastline in the past 35 years. Half of it has been lost since 1997.

Life Disappears

Shishmaref is very far away from other places. It has no roads. The town has 10 dog teams. Schools teach children the Inupiaq language.

Shishmaref has many natural resources. Its people hunt and fish to get food. Along Alaska's coast, however, people worry that the animals and fish they eat may disappear.

"Is it practical to stand and fight our Mother Ocean?" the mayor of one Alaskan town says. "Or do we surrender and move?"

▼ **Kids in Shishmaref see how global warming affects their town.**

Vincent J. Musi/Aurora

Stay or Go?

Shishmaref is falling into the ocean. Houses are falling down. Waves washed away the school playground. Eskimo people may need to move their villages away from the ocean. The people of Shishmaref decided to move to a new place called Tin Creek. Tin Creek is 12 miles away. This was a difficult decision.

One Eskimo mother is also a town leader. She said, "Shishmaref is where it is because of what the ocean, rivers, streams, and the land provide to us. We are hunters and we are gatherers. We have been here for countless generations. We value our way of life. It provides for our very existence."

Al Grillo/AP Photo

▲ **Shishmaref is falling into the ocean.**

The Future

It may be very expensive to move Shishmaref. The U.S. Army Corps of Engineers thinks it may cost about $1 million for each person. Still, Shishmaref's people want to stay together.

Rising sea levels may wash away more sea towns in the United States. It will cost a lot to move people to new places. Communities may break apart. We do not know if more villages in Alaska will move away from the ocean. People must make tough decisions to face these problems in the future. —*Margot Roosevelt*

▼ **Village leaders are worried. They may lose their traditional way of life.**

Vincent J. Musi/Aurora

87

Description Writing Frame

Use the Writing Frame to orally summarize "Landforms Can Change."

Earth's landforms can change.

Water can change landforms. As rivers flow downhill, they _____

_____ .

Rivers can form a delta by _____

_____ .

Waves can also change landforms. **For example**, waves _____

_____ .

Wind can change landforms, too. **For example**, wind carries _____

_____ that scratch the surface of rocks.

Wind can also blow _____ .

Ice, such as _____ , can also change landforms.

When glaciers move, they tear _____ .
This movement can widen, and deepen, a valley into a U-shape.

Use the Writing Frame to write the summary on another sheet
of paper. Be sure to include the **bold** signal words. Keep this as
a model of this Text Structure.

Critical Thinking

1 Water, waves, ice and _____ can change the shape of landforms.

    A. wind

    B. sun

    C. cliffs

2 Find the sentences in "Alaska Has a Problem" that tell a decision the people of Shishmaref made. Discuss it with a partner.

3 Point to the place in "Landforms Can Change" that gives an example of a quick way landforms can change.

4 Choose your favorite photo from "Landforms Can Change." Write a new caption for it and tell it to a partner.

Captions help the reader tell how similar pictures are different.

Digital Learning

For a list of links and activities that relate to this Science standard, visit the California Treasures Web site at www.macmillanmh.com to access the Content Readers resources.

Have students view the e-Review "Landforms: Changing Over Time." In addition, distribute copies of the Translated Concept Summaries in Spanish, Chinese, Hmong, Khmer, and Vietnamese.

Weathering

Rocks are constantly changing. Rocks break into smaller pieces because of freezing and thawing, plants, wind, and pressure. The breakdown of rocks is called **weathering**.

In **chemical weathering,** rocks break down because chemicals change the rocks. Oxygen, acids, and carbon dioxide react with minerals in rock.

Physical weathering happens when wind and rain break down rocks. Physical weathering changes the size and shape of rocks. Here are four causes of physical weathering.

▲ Hematite contains iron. Sometimes iron mixes with oxygen. Then things with iron rust and break down.

Physical weathering formed the North Window Arch in Arches National Park, Utah. ▼

90

These roots will split the rock apart.

Freezing and Thawing

Water from rain or melted snow enters small cracks in rocks. Water expands, or takes up more space, when it freezes. It causes cracks to get bigger. Then the water may thaw, or melt. The freezing and thawing repeats over time. In time, the rocks break apart.

Plants

The roots of a plant can grow through small cracks in rocks. The roots grow larger. Then they make the cracks bigger. Finally the rocks break apart.

Exfoliation

Some rocks, like granite, are buried. They change when heavy layers of rock wear away. The outer layers of the granite expand more than layers below. These top layers peel off like the layers of an onion. This process is called exfoliation.

Abrasion

Winds can also change rock. Winds that carry sand can break down the softer parts of rocks. The sharp edges of sand wear away rock. This process is called wind abrasion.

The Old Man of the Mountain

A much-loved natural sculpture teaches an important lesson about the forces that shape Earth's surface.

▲ In the 1930s, visitors look at the Old Man of the Mountain.

The Old Man of the Mountain was a rock formation in Franconia Notch, New Hampshire. This rock formation looked like a face seen from the side. The face measured 40 feet from chin to forehead. It was 25 feet wide.

Thousands of people visited the Old Man. New Hampshire named him the state symbol in 1945. In 2000, the U.S. Mint issued the New Hampshire quarter with a picture of the Old Man.

In 1805, some surveyors said they were the first to see the Old Man. But in the 1600s, Native Americans told stories of the mountain with a face.

▼ Native Americans saw the Old Man first.

A 12,000-Year-Old Man

The story of the Old Man of the Mountain starts 12,000 years ago. This was during the last ice age. A huge ice sheet covered North America. Then the ice sheet melted. It molded the mountains that made Franconia Notch. It carved the Old Man in the rock.

The End of the Old Man

Over the years, natural forces have been causing the Old Man to crumble.

◄ **In 2003, the granite slabs fell. The Old Man was gone.**

The Old Man was made of five slabs, or pieces, of granite. A long, narrow cavern, or cave, was behind its chin. Only about 2 feet of the chin was connected to the cliff. The other four slabs of granite held the chin in place. It was amazing that the chin did not fall.

Rain and snow blew into the cavern and other cracks between the five slabs. The water between the slabs froze and expanded. This pushed the slabs apart.

Finally, on May 3, 2003, the rock behind the Old Man's chin moved a little. Then the chin fell down. The rest of the Old Man fell immediately after.

We Remember the Old Man

People still come to the park today. They want to remember the Old Man. You can find pictures of the Old Man on the Internet. —*Lisa Jo Rudy*

Sculptures in Nature

You can see sculptures made by natural forces in many parts of the world. Here are two examples in the United States.

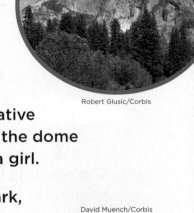

Robert Glusic/Corbis

Half Dome, Yosemite National Park, California: This granite dome is more than 4,700 feet above the Yosemite Valley. Native Americans believe the dome shows the face of a girl.

David Muench/Corbis

Arches National Park, Utah: This is a high desert area. It has many rock formations. Wind, water, and other forces carved these rocks over millions of years.

Problem/Solution Writing Frame

Use the Writing Frame to orally summarize "The Old Man of the Mountain."

The forces of nature crumbled the Old Man of the Mountain in Franconia Notch, New Hampshire.

This is a problem for many people **because** they _____

_____ .

This problem occurred because _____

_____

and pushed the slabs apart.

To help solve the problem, people _____

_____ .

You can also look on the _____

_____ .

The result is that people can still enjoy the Old Man of the Mountain.

Use the Writing Frame to write the summary on another sheet of paper. Be sure to include the **bold** signal words. Keep this as a model of this Text Structure.

Critical Thinking

1 Abrasion, exfoliation and freezing are all examples
   of _____.

   A. thawing

   B. chemical weathering

   C. physical weathering

2 Find the section in "The Old Man of the Mountain" that tells what
   carved the rock formation.

3 Sometimes the outer layers of rock peel. Find the word in
   "Weathering" that names this process.

4 Look at the photograph at the bottom of page
   90. Discuss what happened to the landform
   with a partner.

Photographs provide
visual examples of facts
that appear in a text.

Digital Learning

For a list of links and activities that relate to this Science standard,
visit the California Treasures Web site at www.macmillanmh.com to
access the Content Readers resources.

Have students view the e-Review "Weathering."

In addition, distribute copies of the Translated Concept Summaries in
Spanish, Chinese, Hmong, Khmer, and Vietnamese.

CALIFORNIA IN THE WORLD

How can you describe the location of California? California is part of the United States. The United States, in turn, is part of a continent, or large piece of land, called North America. Find North America on the map.

North America, in turn, is part of the Western Hemisphere. A **hemisphere** is half of a sphere, or globe. Earth is divided into four hemispheres. They are the Northern, Southern, Eastern, and Western hemispheres.

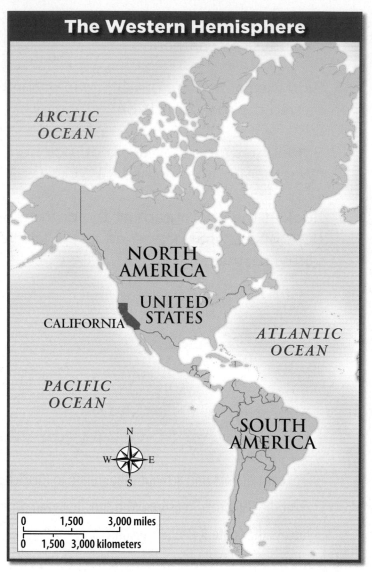

The Western Hemisphere

ARCTIC OCEAN

NORTH AMERICA

UNITED STATES

CALIFORNIA

ATLANTIC OCEAN

PACIFIC OCEAN

SOUTH AMERICA

N
W   E
S

0   1,500   3,000 miles
0   1,500   3,000 kilometers

Geographers use maps with grids to describe the address of every place on Earth. **Grids** are lines that cross on a map. The grid system is based on two sets of lines. These lines are called **latitude** and **longitude**.

Lines of latitude measure how far north or south a place is from the equator. Lines of latitude are also called **parallels**. You label parallels north of the equator "N." You label parallels south of the equator "S."

Lines of longitude measure distance east or west. Lines of longitude are also called **meridians**. You start at the prime meridian when you measure distance from east or west. You label meridians east of the prime meridian "E." You label meridians west of the prime meridian "W."

Lines of latitude and longitude measure distance in **degrees**. The equator is 0 degrees latitude. The prime meridian is 0 degrees longitude. The symbol for degrees is °.

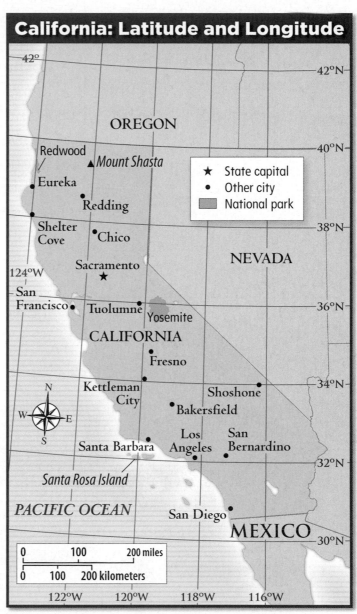

California: Latitude and Longitude

97

National Parks in California

California is a big state. It is 770 miles from north to south. That is almost 10 degrees of latitude. This long state has a lot of geographic diversity. You can see this diversity in the many different national parks in California.

Each national park has its own special features.

California's National Parks are:

- Channel Islands National Park
- Death Valley National Park
- Joshua Tree National Park
- Lassen Volcanic National Park
- Point Reyes National Seashore
- Redwood National Park
- Sequoia & Kings Canyon National Parks
- Yosemite National Park

Here is information about two of California's magnificent national parks.

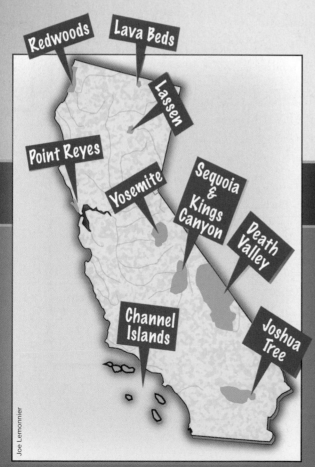

Joe Lemonnier

Cities Share Latitude

Sacramento is the capital of California. It is just above 38°N latitude. You can pass through other cities with the same latitude if you travel east from Sacramento. You can pass through or near these places: Washington, D.C.; Lisbon, Portugal; Ankara, Turkey; Tianjin, China; and Pyongyang, North Korea.

Lassen Volcanic National Park

Lassen Volcanic National Park is in northeastern California. There are more than 30 volcanoes in this park. Lassen Peak is the largest. It erupted last in 1915. It spewed ash for 200 miles. Scientists check for signs of new eruptions.

Molten, or melted, rock is near volcanoes. In Lassen Park, the molten rock is just below the surface. The heat makes fumaroles (vents for steam and volcanic gas), mud pots, boiling pools, and steaming ground. Water heated by molten rock makes the steam.

Altrendo Travel/Getty Images

▲ **Lassen Park has boiling pools and steaming vents.**

Joshua Tree National Park

Joshua Tree National Park is in the high desert in Southern California. Inside the park are an amazing variety of plants and animals. Wind and rain formed the rocks and sand into strange shapes.

Joshua Tree National Park was named for the Joshua tree. Native Americans made baskets and sandals from the leaves of the twisted, spiky tree. They roasted the seeds and nuts for food. —*Lisa Jo Rudy*

▼ **The Joshua tree lives in the high desert.**

Altrendo Panoramic/Getty Images

99

Description Writing Frame

Use the Writing Frame to orally summarize "National Parks in California."

National parks in California have **many interesting features**.

For example, there are volcanoes at _____

_____ .

In 1915, _____ .

Another interesting feature of Lassen Park is the steaming

_____ .

The steam comes from _____

_____ .

There are many interesting trees in California's National parks.

For example, the twisted, spiky _____

was used by _____

to make _____ .

You can see one if you visit _____ .

Use the Writing Frame to write the summary on another sheet of paper. Be sure to include **bold** signal words. Keep this as a model of this Text Structure.

Critical Thinking

1. Lines that cross on a map are called _____.

   A. grids

   B. hemispheres

   C. degrees

2. Find the phrase in "National Parks in California" that explains what a fumarole is.

3. Show a partner the place in "California in the World" that tells how you can describe the location of California.

4. Review the map on page 97. Find the longitude and latitude that is near where you live.

A compass rose shows north, south, east, and west directions.

Digital Learning

For a list of links and activities that relate to this History/Social Science standard, visit the California Treasures Web site at www.macmillanmh.com to access the Content Readers resources. Have students read "Yosemite National Park."

THE PHYSICAL REGIONS OF CALIFORNIA

California has four physical regions. They are: mountains, valleys, the coast, and deserts. Each region affects human activity in different ways.

Mountains

There are mountains in every part of California. They are the most common landform in the state. They cover more than half the land.

The mountains supply important natural resources such as water, wood, and minerals. Major **industries** developed around these resources. An industry is all the businesses that make one type of good or provide one type of service.

Tourism is an important industry in California. **Tourists** are people who travel to see new sights. Tourists from around the world visit California's mountains.

Valleys

California's Central Valley is one of the biggest **valleys** in the world. A valley is a low area between mountains.

The Central Valley is in the middle of four different mountain ranges. It is formed from two valleys. The Sacramento Valley is in the north and the San Joaquin Valley is in the south.

The Central Valley has **fertile** land. Fertile land has rich soil that produces crops easily.

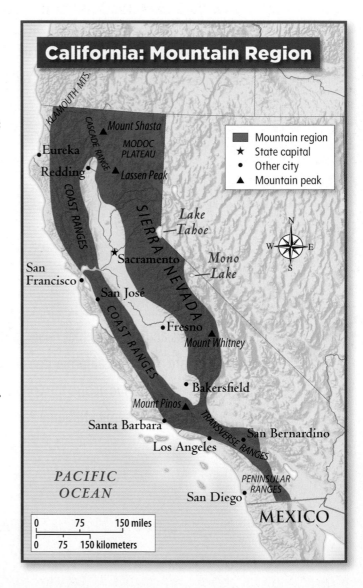

California: Mountain Region

- ■ Mountain region
- ★ State capital
- ● Other city
- ▲ Mountain peak

KLAMOUTH MTS.
CASCADE RANGE
MODOC PLATEAU
Mount Shasta
Eureka
Redding
Lassen Peak
COAST RANGES
SIERRA NEVADA
Lake Tahoe
Mono Lake
Sacramento
San Francisco
San José
Fresno
Mount Whitney
COAST RANGES
Bakersfield
Mount Pinos
TRANSVERSE RANGES
Santa Barbara
San Bernardino
Los Angeles
PACIFIC OCEAN
PENINSULAR RANGES
San Diego
MEXICO

0 75 150 miles
0 75 150 kilometers

The Central Valley is one of the world's most productive agricultural regions today. **Agriculture** is the business of growing crops and raising animals.

The Coast

About three out of four people in California live in the coastal region. They live near the mountains of the Coast Ranges or in the coastal plains of Southern California.

Californians enjoy the warm and pleasant climate of the coast. They also enjoy the ocean. Millions of tourists go to California's beautiful coast every year. Fishing boats in California catch much of the salmon, crab, and other seafood that we eat. California's coastal cities are centers of international business and shipping.

Deserts

California's desert region is made of three deserts: the Colorado Desert, the Mojave Desert, and the Great Basin. These deserts may have no rain for months.

A desert region can also be very hot. Summer temperatures are often over 100 degrees Fahrenheit. Winter temperatures are often below freezing.

In the 1800s few people lived in California's deserts. People had to survive with very little water.

Now things have changed because of **technology**. Technology is the use of skills, tools, and machinery to meet people's needs. **Irrigation** is one product of technology. Irrigation is the use of ditches and pipes to bring water to dry land. Now people can live in hot, dry places.

The Imperial Valley is part of the Colorado Desert. It became fertile after it was irrigated. Now farmers grow fruits and vegetables there.

California: Desert Region

Desert region
National park
★ State capital
• Other city

San José
GREAT BASIN
NEVADA
Fresno
Death Valley
Bakersfield
MOJAVE DESERT
Santa Barbara
Barstow
Mojave
Los Angeles
Joshua Tree
PACIFIC OCEAN
Palm Springs
Salton Sea
0 50 100 miles
0 50 100 kilometers
COLORADO DESERT
IMPERIAL VALLEY
San Diego

Vacation in Death Valley

People ride bicycles in Death Valley.

SCPhotos/Alamy

Death Valley National Park is the largest national park in California. About 1 million visitors come to the 3.3 million hot, dry acres in Death Valley.

White Gold

People came to Death Valley in the 1800s to try to find gold, silver, and copper. Borax became the real treasure. It was known as white gold. People used it in cleaning products. Borax is a mineral found under the ground. In Death Valley, people scraped it off the surface of rocks.

Today, visitors come to Death Valley to see the natural beauty. They can hike or drive to see fantastic landforms.

Sand Dunes Near Stovepipe Wells

Desert winds dropped off grains of sand here. The sand began as solid rock. The dunes and flat sands cover 15 square miles.

Devil's Golf Course

Wind and rain carve salt into amazing pointed shapes. The salt is from ancient saltwater lakes.

Courtesy Death Valley National Park

Mule trains hauled borax out of Death Valley.

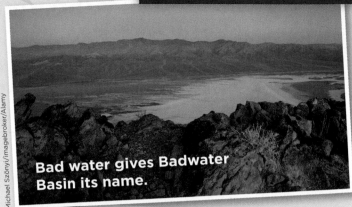

Bad water gives Badwater Basin its name.

Michael Szönyi/imagebroker/Alamy

Badwater Basin

Badwater Basin is the lowest place in North America. It is 282 feet below sea level. You cannot drink the water.

Ubehebe Crater

This crater is over half a mile wide. It is 770 feet deep. 4,000 years ago, magma (hot, liquid underground rock) rose up into cold, shallow groundwater. The mixture changed into steam. Then it exploded. The Ubehebe Crater formed.

The mixture of hot magma and cold water exploded. This caused the crater.

Terry Wall/Alamy

Artist's Drive

The rocks along Artist's Drive in the Black Mountains get amazing colors from minerals. Reds and yellows are from iron. Green is from mica. —*Susan Moger*

Volcanic rocks get their colors from minerals.

Michael Szönyi/imagebroker/Alamy

Amy Raedts/Alamy

The Mysterious Moving Rocks in Death Valley

Some rocks in a dry basin called Racetrack Playa look like they have moved. There are long trails in the dirt behind them. Maybe the rocks moved and left the tracks. No one knows.

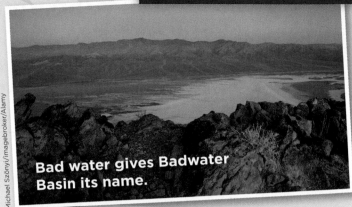
TIME FOR KIDS

105

Problem/Solution Writing Frame

**Use the Writing Frame to orally summarize
"The Physical Regions of California."**

California has four physical regions. They are: _____

_____ .

Sometimes, California's deserts have no rain for months. In the

past **this was a problem because** _____

_____ .

Today there is irrigation. Now the Imperial Valley is _____

_____ .

A desert region can also be very hot. Summer temperatures are _____

_____ .

Today people use technology to stay cool. **The result** is that

people can _____ .

Use the Writing Frame to write the summary on another sheet of
paper. Be sure to include **bold** signal words. Keep this as a model
of this Text Structure.

Critical Thinking

1 A low area between mountains is a _____.

   A. coast

   B. desert

   C. valley

2 Point to the word in "The Physical Regions of California" for people who travel to see new sights.

3 Locate the section in "Vacation in Death Valley" that explains white gold.

4 Orally create a caption for your favorite photo in "Vacation in Death Valley." Share your caption with a partner.

Photographs provide visual examples of facts in a text.

Digital Learning

For a list of links and activities that relate to this History/Social Science standard, visit the California Treasures Web site at www.macmillanmh.com to access the Content Readers resources. Have students view the video "The Golden State–Our Home."

LAND MEETS WATER

California's coast runs 1,300 miles from Oregon to Mexico. This narrow strip along the Pacific Ocean is the most crowded region in California.

In Northern California, the coast is rocky and the water is rough. Some mountains come directly to the ocean.

In Southern California there is a flat plain along the coast. It has sandy beaches and warm weather all year.

Southern California does not rain much. Many Southern Californians enjoy outdoor activities such as surfing, sailing, and biking.

Two large cities are located along the coast of Southern California—San Diego and Los Angeles. They are two of the most populated cities in the United States. These cities have large businesses. They are exciting places to live in or visit.

This bird is a puffin. It lives along California's coast. ▶

Avalon harbor on Santa Catalina island ▼

Northern California is also a good place to live in or visit. The Bay Area is the region around San Francisco Bay. It has the largest number of people on the northern coast. San Francisco and Oakland are two big cities here. Silicon Valley is a center of the computer industry in the Bay Area.

In the valleys north of San Francisco the climate is good for growing grapes. Farther north the coast is rugged. Thick evergreen forests grow there. Logging, or cutting down trees for wood, is a major industry here.

The coast of California is famous for its earthquakes. An **earthquake** is a shaking of the ground.

Do you know what causes earthquakes? Earth's surface is made of enormous **plates**. These plates grind against one another. Sometimes two plates slide quickly against each other. You feel these plates slide when there is an earthquake.

Two of Earth's plates meet at the San Andreas Fault in California. A fault is the crack in the ground where plates meet.

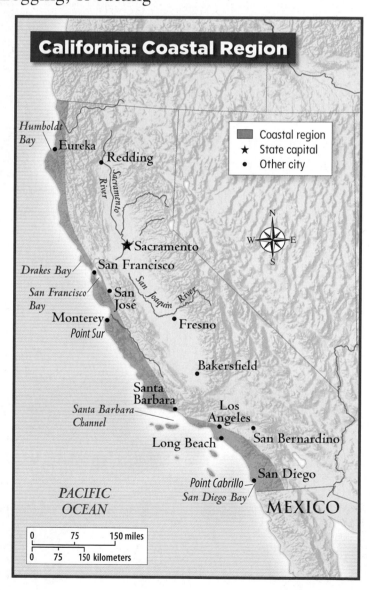

California: Coastal Region

Humboldt Bay
Eureka
Redding
Sacramento River
★ Sacramento
Drakes Bay
San Francisco
San Francisco Bay
San José
Monterey
Point Sur
San Joaquin River
Fresno
Bakersfield
Santa Barbara
Santa Barbara Channel
Los Angeles
Long Beach
San Bernardino
Point Cabrillo
San Diego
San Diego Bay
PACIFIC OCEAN
MEXICO

Coastal region
★ State capital
• Other city

0   75   150 miles
0   75   150 kilometers

EARTHQUAKES
and Buildings

Earthquakes happen often in California. Even small earthquakes can make buildings fall down. However, there are new ways to make buildings safer.

Earthquakes make buildings sway, or move back and forth. Buildings that can sway back and forth a little bit are safer in an earthquake.

Safe Airports
The San Francisco International Airport was built to stay safe from earthquakes.

Steel balls help columns move in an earthquake.

There are 267 columns that support the airport. Each column is on a wide steel ball. Each steel ball sits in a base shaped like a bowl. Each base is connected to the ground.

The balls roll around in their bases when the ground shakes. The columns move a little, but do not fall down. The balls roll back to the center of their bases after the earthquake. The building is normal again.

◀ A small earthquake can destroy a big building.

Skyscrapers Shake

If a skyscraper falls during an earthquake, it can kill hundreds of people. However, skyscrapers are flexible. They can bend. Some move like ocean waves. People inside the building get hurt. We need to build skyscrapers so they move all in one piece. Then people inside will be safe.

The TransAmerica Pyramid in San Francisco looks like a triangle. It is wide at the bottom and narrow at the top. Slanted rods at the base support the building. They support the building during any earthquake.

We Can Fix Old Cities

Many buildings in California are not earthquake-proof, or safe. We can make them safe from earthquakes. We can bolt houses to their foundations. We can use flexible gas pipes that do not break and cause fires. We cannot stop an earthquake. However, we can build safer cities. —*Lisa Jo Rudy*

▼ **We can make old structures stay safe during an earthquake.**

Lacy Atkins/AP Photo

The TransAmerica Pyramid is made to stay safe during an earthquake. ▶

AM Corporation/Alamy

111

Compare/Contrast Writing Frame

**Use the Writing Frame to orally summarize
"Land Meets Water."**

The coast of California has mountains. Some mountains in

Northern California _____ .

The coast is rocky and _____ .

However, in Southern California there is _____

_____ .

California's northern and southern coasts have large cities. **However**,

San Diego and Los Angeles are two of _____

_____ .

In northern California, the most crowded region is _____

_____ .

They differ in climate and geography, but the northern and southern

coasts are **both** _____ .

Use the Writing Frame to write the summary on another sheet of
paper. Be sure to include **bold** signal words. Keep this as a model
of this Text Structure.

Critical Thinking

1. Earthquakes happen because of the sliding of _____.

   A. plates

   B. coasts

   C. mountains

2. Find the sentence in "Land Meets Water" that tells how long California's coastline is.

3. Show a partner the paragraph in "Earthquakes and Buildings" that explains how the San Francisco International Airport is built for earthquakes.

4. Review the map on page 109. Point to cities on the coast. Discuss your answer with a partner.

> Labels identify cities, states, rivers, and other land features on a map.

Digital Learning

For a list of links and activities that relate to this History/Social Science standard, visit the California Treasures Web site at www.macmillanmh.com to access the Content Readers resources. Have students read the Biography "John Muir."

THE FIRST PEOPLE OF CALIFORNIA

There were already millions of people living in North and South America when the first Europeans arrived. More than 300,000 Native Americans lived in California.

Over time, the early people of California learned to live with the natural resources of different climates. People used their nearby resources to make clothes, tools, and homes wherever they settled.

Groups near the ocean developed tools to catch and dry fish. People in valleys with oak trees found ways to make acorns into flour.

Over time, the Native Americans of California molded at least 100 different cultures, or ways of life. Each had its own language, crafts, beliefs, and traditions.

Geographers divide the 100 groups into six regions called **culture areas**. The groups living in each area have cultures that are alike in some ways. The six culture areas are Northwestern, Northeastern, Central, Great Basin, Southern, and Colorado River.

We do not know how often people traveled out of their local areas. We do know that they traded with one another. We also know that most of the Native Americans in California spoke at least two languages.

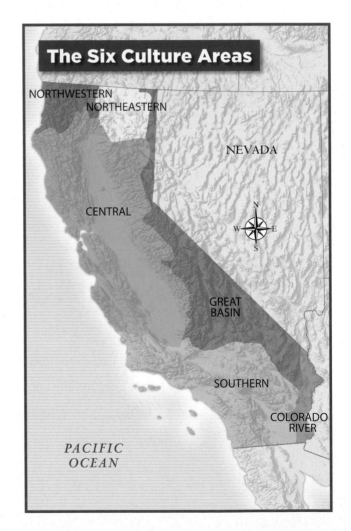

The Six Culture Areas

NORTHWESTERN
NORTHEASTERN
NEVADA
CENTRAL
GREAT BASIN
SOUTHERN
COLORADO RIVER
PACIFIC OCEAN

The Yokuts and many other peoples lived in the Central culture area. The Yokuts lived in the San Joaquin Valley and the foothills of the Sierra Nevada. They had many natural resources. The many tall oak trees in the valley and the foothills were the most important. They produced tons of acorns every fall.

Yokuts men hunted a lot. They also helped harvest acorns in the fall. They shook the branches to make the nuts fall. Then the women and children picked up the nuts. Then, they packed the nuts away in a storage house.

Yokuts communities burned parts of their land each year. The fires made ash. The ash made the soil fertile for growing crops. The fires also cleared away plants. Then there was more land for animals to hunt, such as deer and antelope. This was just one way that Native Americans practiced **land management**, or care of the land.

The Northern Paiute lived in the Great Basin culture area. This area included the Sierra Nevada and Death Valley. This territory is now the eastern border of California, next to Nevada.

There were no oak trees to supply acorns or green valleys for hunting in this area. However the Northern Paiute found other sources of food.

These food sources depended on the season. So, people had to move each season. In early summer, water from the mountains created shallow lakes. People found fish and water birds in these lakes. Later in the year, people climbed the foothills of the Sierra Nevada. They hunted mountain sheep there. They found places to catch hares, or rabbits, on the way.

The economy of the Northern Paiute was based on skillful hunting and gathering. People traded with other groups for foods such as dried fish to add to their resources.

▼ **A Yokuts woman makes acorn into flour.**

Save the Salmon!

When they were 14 years old, Kayla Carpenter and Erika Chase saw 64,000 salmon die. The fish died in the Klamath River in California. Kayla and Erika knew a lot about this river. They grew up fishing in the river. They are Yurok and Hupa Indians. Their communities depended on salmon. They had eaten this fish for thousands of years.

Kayla and Erika described how their community felt. They said, "Young and old cried in sadness and despair. We fear that with a few more years like this, our generation will see wild salmon become extinct in our rivers."

▲ **Kayla and Erika**

We Can Make a Difference

"As Indian people and as young people, our future depends on the defense of our natural resources. We can all make a difference. All it takes is the spirit to act."
—Kayla Carpenter and Erika Chase

Water for Farms or Fish?

Dams have slowed down the Klamath River over 40 years. Dams divide the river water. Much of it goes to strawberry and cotton fields in the desert. Not enough is left for fish.

This dam on the Klamath River has serious effects for salmon.

The First Salmon Run Relay

In 2003, a year after the salmon died, Kayla and Erika organized the first Salmon Run Relay. Kayla and Erika wanted to educate people and get them involved. They hoped to get people to exercise and eat healthful foods.

Courtesy Kayla Carpenter

▲ **People run in the Salmon Run Relay.**

Volunteer runners carried a wooden fish 41 miles. The wooden fish was a symbol for the salmon that swim in the river. The salmon come up river to lay eggs. The young fish swim to the ocean. The runners started at the mouth of the river. They followed the salmon's route. "The runners took on the salmon's struggle to call the world's attention," Erika said. Now the Salmon Run Relay happens every year.

The Award

In 2005, Kayla and Erika received the Earth Island Institute's Brower Youth Award. This is the highest environmental award for young people in the United States. —*Susan Moger*

The Hupa, Yurok, and Karuk Indians

These Northern California Indians have lived along the Klamath and Trinity Rivers for thousands of years. Salmon are important in their cultures. The Indians caught salmon in the spring and fall as the fish returned to the river to spawn, or lay eggs.

The Yurok, Hupa, and Karuk have ceremonies to conserve this natural resource. The Salmon Run Relay includes a salmon ceremony. It is based on the ancient rituals.

Catherine Karnow/Corbis

A Northern California Indian with two salmon

117

Problem/Solution Writing Frame

Use the Writing Frame to orally summarize "Save the Salmon!"

Kayla Carpenter and Erika Chase had a **problem**. _____

_____ in the Klamath River.

This was a problem for the Yurok and Hupa Indians **because**

_____

_____ .

The problem occurred because _____

_____ .

Only a small amount of water is left for fish. Kayla and

Erika helped **solve this problem when they** _____

_____

to educate people and get them involved.

Use the Writing Frame to write the summary on another sheet of paper. Be sure to include **bold** signal words. Keep this as a model of this Text Structure.

Critical Thinking

1 Which area is not one of the culture areas?

   A. Southwestern

   B. Northeastern

   C. Great Basin

2 Find the paragraph in "The First People of California" that explains land management. Discuss with a partner how Native Americans practiced land management.

3 Locate the section in "Save the Salmon!" that describes the route the runners follow.

4 Review the photograph on page 116. Discuss with a partner if the dams are helpful or harmful.

Photographs and captions give visual examples that help explain the text.

Digital Learning

For a list of links and activities that relate to this History/Social Science standard, visit the California Treasures Web site at www.macmillanmh.com to access the Content Readers resources. Have students read the "A Young Native American's Life in California."

EXPLORATIONS OF CABRILLO

In 1542 the **viceroy**, or ruler, of New Spain told Juan Rodriguez Cabrillo to explore the coast of California. New Spain was the Spanish colony in North America. It is now Mexico, Central America, and the United States.

Cabrillo was a conquistador and a sea captain. **Conquistadors** were soldiers who took land by force.

On June 27, 1542, Cabrillo and his crew set sail with two small ships. On September 28, 1542, the ships sailed into a bay. Cabrillo named the bay San Miguel. Later it was renamed San Diego. For six days they explored the land and met the local Kumeyaay people. Then they continued north. They sailed to the place we call Santa Catalina Island.

Cabrillo traveled farther north along the coast. They met Native Americans on the islands of San Miguel, Santa Cruz, and Santa Rosa outside the Santa Barbara Channel.

Cabrillo claimed the land he found for New Spain. He called it "Alta California," or upper California. Cabrillo founded a town, which he named "Pueblo de las Canoas," the Town of the Canoes.

Cabrillo reached the Channel Islands in 1542.

The Beginning of New Spain

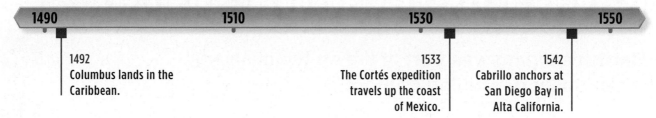

1490	1510	1530	1550

1492
Columbus lands in the Caribbean.

1533
The Cortés expedition travels up the coast of Mexico.

1542
Cabrillo anchors at San Diego Bay in Alta California.

Cabrillo's **expedition**, or journey of exploration, went into the Santa Barbara Channel. Cabrillo and his men saw a Native American town with large adobe houses on one of the islands.

The people Cabrillo met were the Chumash. They told Cabrillo that there was a large river flowing into the sea farther north. The explorers set sail, but were held back a month by bad weather.

In time the Chumash on the Channel Islands wanted the explorers to leave their land. On December 24, 1542, the Chumash attacked Cabrillo's men. Cabrillo broke his arm as he tried to rescue his men. He died from the injury later.

Before he died, Cabrillo asked Bartolomé Ferrelo, his chief pilot, to lead the expedition. Ferrelo ordered the men to bury Cabrillo on the island where he died. Today that island is called San Miguel Island.

Ferrelo headed north but was delayed by bad weather. Soon after, another storm damaged the ships. Ferrelo ended the expedition. Historians think he had reached the border of present-day Oregon.

Cabrillo and Ferrelo discovered many harbors of Baja and Alta California on their expedition. Historians identified 70 locations from their journals.

This statue of Cabrillo is in San Diego.

121

CALIFORNIA AND CATTLE

Cattle ranching was part of life on the missions when Spain controlled California.

The year was 1769. The place was Baja California. This was the southern part of Spain's colony north of Mexico. Spain was in charge, but Russians were moving south from Alaska. The king of Spain was worried. He had to hold California and build his empire.

The king's solution to this problem was a man, Father Junipero Serra. Serra was a Catholic priest. He had worked in Mexico for many years. Serra landed his boats in San Diego, California. He brought several hundred head of cattle.

Serra Builds Missions

Serra's goal was to build missions. Missions were buildings where priests lived and held religious services. Farms and ranches nearby produced food for the people who lived in the mission.

Serra Brings American Indians to the Missions

Serra wanted to bring Native Americans to the missions. He wanted them to be Christians. He hoped they would support the Spanish.

Father Junipero Serra

Lake County Museum/Corbis

▼ **This is the Mission San Carlos Borromeo del Rio Carmelo, in Carmel, California today.**

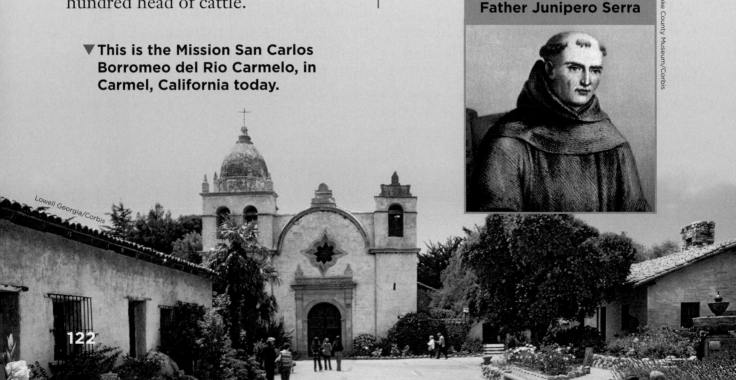

Lowell Georgia/Corbis

Lake County Museum/Corbis

◀ **Mission Santa Clara de Asis, in Santa Clara**

Corbis

▲ **Mission Indians make rope and baskets.**

Serra built nine missions along the California coast. He and other priests worked to bring in Native Americans. Native Americans learned about Christianity and the Spanish language at the missions. They also learned about ranching and cattle.

Cattle Ranching Is Popular

California weather was perfect for raising cattle. In 1774 there were about 350 head of longhorn cattle in California. By 1834 there were 396,000!

The Spanish missions stopped ranching when California became part of the United States in 1848. However, longhorn cattle became part of California life. Cow skins (leather) were worth money. Californians traded with ships' captains for things they needed.

The End of an Era

In 1864 there was a terrible drought. Many of the cattle died. A few years later ranchers bought more cattle. Then their ranches were back in business. Even so, the golden era of ranching was over. —*Lisa Jo Rudy*

▼ **Longhorn cattle were an important part of California's economy.**

DLILLC/Corbis

Sequence Writing Frame

Use the Writing Frame to orally summarize "Explorations of Cabrillo."

In June of 1542, the viceroy of New Spain _____

_____ .

On September 28, **1542**, Cabrillo's _____

_____ . Cabrillo named the bay San Miguel.

Next, they explored _____

and met _____ .

After he left San Miguel, Cabrillo and his crew traveled north to

the islands of _____

_____ .

On December 24, **1542**, _____

_____ . While trying to rescue them,

Cabrillo broke his arm. **Later** _____

_____ .

Use the Writing Frame to write the summary on another sheet of paper. Be sure to include the **bold** signal word. Keep this as a model of this Text Structure.

Critical Thinking

1. The Spanish word for soldiers who took land by force is _____ .

   A. viceroy

   B. conquistadors

   C. expedition

2. Find the sentence in "California and Cattle" that explains what missions were.

3. Locate the section in "California and Cattle" that describes the importance of Native Americans to the missions.

   Time lines show historical events in the order they occurred.

4. Review the time line on page 121. Point to where you think Ferrelo led the expedition. Discuss with a partner.

Digital Learning

For a list of links and activities that relate to this History/Social Science standard, visit the California Treasures Web site at www.macmillanmh.com to access the Content Readers resources. Have students view "Early California History."

THE MEXICAN WAR FOR INDEPENDENCE

For 300 years Spain sent officials across the Atlantic Ocean to rule New Spain. Mexican colonists did not want to be ruled by faraway Spain. They learned how the United States had won its freedom from Great Britain. The Mexicans wanted their freedom, too. In 1810 they went to war with Spain to win independence.

The Mexican War for Independence lasted 11 years. Mexico was an independent country, free of Spanish rule, when the war finally ended in 1821.

The war in Mexico was far from California. Many people in California did not know that Mexico had won the war until 1822. The Californios, the Mexican people in California, raised their new flag when they heard the news. California was now under Mexico's new government.

Life changed in California. For example, the Mexican government closed the Spanish missions. In the missions, priests taught Native Americans the Christian religion.

The Mexican government made this decision for several reasons. The missions were on valuable land. The Californios wanted this land for ranches and farms. Also, many Mexicans believed that Native Americans were not treated fairly at the missions. Some Native Americans led revolts against the missions. The new government's leaders said that all people were equal.

In 1834 California's new governor, José Figueroa, ordered the missions closed. He wanted to stop the revolts. Figueroa also gave half the mission lands to the Native Americans who had lived and worked on the land.

Many Californios supported Governor Figueroa's plan. They wanted mission land for themselves. The Mexican government gave out most of the mission lands in larger pieces, known as **land grants**.

Any Mexican citizen could apply for a land grant. However, Californio land owners and soldiers from the presidios (military forts) received most of the first land grants. Native Americans received few.

The Californios turned their new land into more than 500 ranchos. A rancho was a ranch where cattle, horses, and other animals were raised. Mariano Guadalupe Vallejo was one of the richest **rancheros**, or ranch owners. He became an army commander and went into politics.

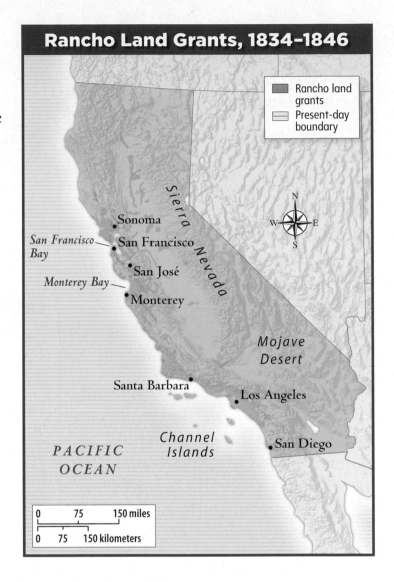

Rancho Land Grants, 1834–1846

Rancho land grants
Present-day boundary

Sierra Nevada

Sonoma
San Francisco Bay
San Francisco
San José
Monterey Bay
Monterey

Mojave Desert

Santa Barbara
Los Angeles

Channel Islands

San Diego

PACIFIC OCEAN

0   75   150 miles
0   75   150 kilometers

Ranchos of California

Cattle-ranching was big business in California in the 1800s.

▲ The brand for "San Juan Capistano"

After Mexico won independence from Spain in 1821, the Catholic missions lost land and power. Huge areas of land were granted to wealthy families. These areas were turned into *ranchos* (ranches) for cattle-raising. The owners were called *rancheros*.

California Native Americans did most of the work on the ranchos. Some became skilled cowhands, called *vaqueros*. A typical rancho had from 20 to several hundred Native American workers.

These workers were not paid money. They received food, shelter, and clothing instead. Owners often used violence to control them.

Cattle Economy

Ranchos had huge herds of cattle. They had many acres of good grazing land. Cattle from different ranchos often got mixed together because there were no fences. So owners branded their cattle. They burned a mark on every cow's hide to identify its owner.

▼ Vaqueros at work

The Granger Collection

Eventually, the cattle were sorted by owner. Then they were killed. The hides were used to make leather saddles, shoes, and other products. Cattle fat was boiled down into tallow for making soap and candles.

California was still part of Mexico. Traders from the United States and other countries traded factory-made goods for hides and tallow.

Rancho Life

Rich landowners enjoyed a comfortable life. They dedicated their life to family and tradition—and beef. They ate beef for breakfast, lunch, and dinner. Their fun included grizzly bear hunts, bull and bear fighting, and weddings! —*Susan Moger*

Water Resources Center Archives, 410 O'Brien, University of California,

▲ **A rancho in Inyo County, California, 1906**

Prudencia Higuera—We Trade for Toothbrushes

In 1840 Prudencia Higuera, a member of a ranchero family, described how her family traded with a ship from the United States.

My brothers drove [the cattle] to the beach, killed them there, and salted the hides. They [melted] the tallow in some iron kettles. The captain [of the U.S. ship] soon came to our landing in a small boat.

The captain looked over the hides and then asked my father to get into the boat and go to the vessel. [My father] came back the next day, bringing four boat-loads of cloth, axes, shoes, fish-lines, and many new things. My brother traded for four toothbrushes. [They were] the first ones I had ever seen.

Cause/Effect Writing Frame

Use the Writing Frame to orally summarize "Ranchos of California."

In 1821 Mexico won independence from Spain. One **effect** this had

on California was that the Catholic missions _____

_____ .

Because some people received large _____

this caused the rise of a rich group of _____ .

Because the land granted to wealthy families was so large, most

of the work was done by _____ .

This explains why some Indians became _____
called vaqueros.

The workers were not paid money, but they received _____

_____ instead.

Rich landowners enjoyed a comfortable life because other people
did their work for them. **The result was that** rancheros were able to

dedicate _____ .

Use the Writing Frame to write the summary on another sheet of
paper. Be sure to include the **bold** signal words. Keep this as a
model of this Text Structure.

Critical Thinking

1. An area of land the Mexican government gave to Mexicans who settled in California was called a _____.

    A. rancho

    B. land grant

    C. farm

2. Point to the sentence in "Ranchos of California" that explains the word *branded*.

3. Locate the section in "The Mexican War for Independence" that explains who could apply for a land grant.

4. Review the map on page 127 with a partner. Discuss the location of rancho land grants. Where are the most land grants located?

A key or legend helps you interpret the colors or special symbols on a map.

Digital Learning

For a list of links and activities that relate to this History/Social Science standard, visit the California Treasures Web site at www.macmillanmh.com to access the Content Readers resources. Have students read "A Young Person's Life in the 1840s."

THE FUR TRADE

In the early 1800s, Russian fur hunters sailed down the coast of California from Alaska. California was still part of Mexico. In 1812 these fur hunters built Fort Ross about 50 miles north of San Francisco.

The Russians used Fort Ross as a base to hunt sea otters and seals. These animals were valuable for their **pelts**. A pelt is the fur-covered hide of an animal. Fur coats and hats were popular at the time. They were soft, warm, and waterproof.

The Russians were not the only people interested in fur. American **trappers** soon went to California to get beaver pelts. A trapper is someone who catches animals for their fur.

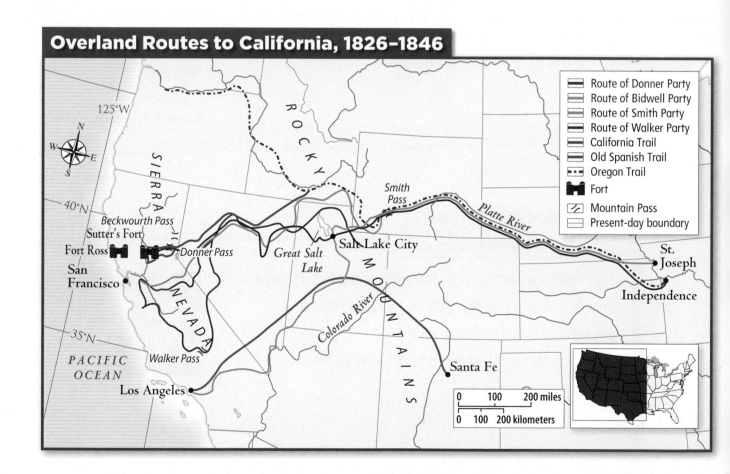

Overland Routes to California, 1826–1846

Many pioneer families walked beside their covered wagons.

Jebediah Strong Smith believed there were many beavers in California. In 1826 he led 15 trappers there. They were the first people from the United States to go to California over land. They left on August 16 from what is now Utah. They traveled southwest through mountains and deserts.

In early October the group reached the Colorado River near California. They made it across the Mojave Desert with the help of Native American guides. On November 27, Smith and the other trappers arrived at Mission San Gabriel.

There they heard that the San Joaquin Valley had many beavers. The Mexican governor thought Smith was an American spy. He ordered Smith to leave California.

In 1839 Johann (John) Sutter arrived in California. Sutter received a land grant in the Sacramento Valley after coming to Monterey. He built a large settlement with a fort.

New settlers to California often stopped at Sutter's Fort. The first people to settle in the area are called **pioneers**. These pioneers came mostly from Eastern states.

Sutter's Fort

John Sutter's businesses were failing. So he left his home in Switzerland in 1834 and went to the United States. In 1838, he joined a trapping party that was going to the Pacific Coast. From Vancouver, he sailed to Hawaii.

In Hawaii, Sutter pretended to be a successful captain in the Swiss Guards. He persuaded important Hawaiians to lend him money. Then he sailed to California with a group of nine Hawaiians.

▲ **John Sutter**

National Gallery of Art, Washington, D.C/SuperStock, Inc.

Sutter builds New Switzerland

In 1839, California was still part of Mexico. Sutter asked the Mexican government for land. The government agreed. Sutter and his Hawaiian friends went up the Sacramento River. They arrived near what is now Sacramento.

Next, Sutter met a large group of Native Americans. He offered them work. Together they worked the land. Sutter called it New Helvetia ("New Switzerland").

In 1840, Sutter started building a fort. The fort protected a growing community that included Mexicans, Hawaiians, and Native Americans. New Helvetia had large herds of cattle and horses. Hunters from the community gathered fur pelts and elk hides. Sutter built a flour mill, a bakery, a blacksmith shop, and a carpenter shop.

Sutter's Fort was completed in 1844. As more settlers arrived, it became known for hospitality.

Gold! The End of Sutter's Fort

Then, in 1847, Sutter started building a sawmill for a man named James Marshall. He was almost finished in 1848, but then Marshall discovered gold in the water.

By 1849, thousands rushed to California to prospect for gold. The Gold Rush hurt Sutter. His workmen quit to look for gold. Gold prospectors stole his land, crops, and animals. He tried to sell goods to the miners, but they cheated him.

Penniless, Sutter left his land to his son, John Jr., and moved to Pennsylvania. John Jr. started the new town of Sacramento. John Sutter had lost the empire he built, but his work lived on. —*Lisa Jo Rudy*

▼ **An 1855 painting of miners at Sutter's Mill**

The Bancroft Library

▼ **Sutter's Fort today**

Robert Holmes/Corbis

An 1849 illustration of Sutter's Fort

The Bancroft Library

135

Compare/Contrast Writing Frame

Use the Writing Frame below to orally summarize "The Fur Trade."

Russian and American settlers were **similar** in many ways. They were

alike because they both wanted _____.

In addition, they both traveled to _____.

In some ways, however, _____ and _____

settlers were **different**. They were **different** because some Russian

fur hunters sailed _____

_____.

However, some American settlers came to California over land

through _____.

Another **difference** was that Russians were hunting _____,

while Americans were hunting _____.

Use the Writing Frame to write the summary on another sheet of
paper. Be sure to include the **bold** signal words. Keep this as a
model of this Text Structure.

Critical Thinking

1 The first people to settle in an area are called _____.

    A. pioneers

    B. trappers

    C. immigrants

2 Locate the sentence in "The Fur Trade" that defines what a pelt is.

3 Reread the paragraph in "Sutter's Fort" that explains the end of Sutter's Fort.

4 Look at the photograph and illustrations on page 135. Discuss with a partner how they support the text.

> Photographs and captions help explain the text.

Digital Learning

For a list of links and activities that relate to this History/Social Science standard, visit the California Treasures Web site at www.macmillanmh.com to access the Content Readers resources. Have students view "Becoming A State."

THEY FOUND GOLD!

On January 24, 1849, men were hard at work on a project for Johann Sutter. Sutter was a Swiss immigrant to Mexican California. The men stood in the American River. Suddenly, one of them spotted something shiny. He said later, "It made my heart thump, for I was certain it was gold."

The news spread around the world. Nearly 80,000 people from around the world came to California to find gold during 1849. They were called **forty-niners**. This rapid movement of people in search of gold is called the **Gold Rush**.

By the spring of 1849, thousands of people wanted to go to California. They chose among several routes.

One route was by sea. It went around South America. The trip took four to eight months by cargo ship. Some travelers paid more money to travel by **clipper ship**. Clipper ships were sleek and fast with many sails. They made the trip in less time.

The ships were crowded. The food was stale or bad. There was not much fresh water. Getting around Cape Horn at the tip of South America was very risky. Storms sank many ships.

Sutter's Mill is where gold was first found in California.

Another route was also by sea, but had a "shortcut." Travelers went by ship to Panama, in Central America. There, they crossed the Isthmus of Panama. An isthmus is a narrow strip of land. People crossed on foot, by mule, and in small boats through swamps and jungles. After they crossed the Isthmus, another ship took them north to San Francisco.

Most travelers chose the cheapest route—overland by wagon train. Travelers could bring horses, cattle, supplies, and household objects.

Bayard Taylor, a forty-niner from New York, arrived in San Francisco. He saw

"Hundreds of tents and houses . . . scattered all over the [hills] . . . buildings of all kinds, begun or half-finished . . . covered with all kinds of signs in all languages. . . . Goods were piled in the open air. . . . The streets were full of people. . . . One knows not whether he is awake or in some wonderful dream."

There were so many people! There were not enough hotels or houses for them. Stores opened up everywhere. Some stores were built in ships that sailors left in the harbor.

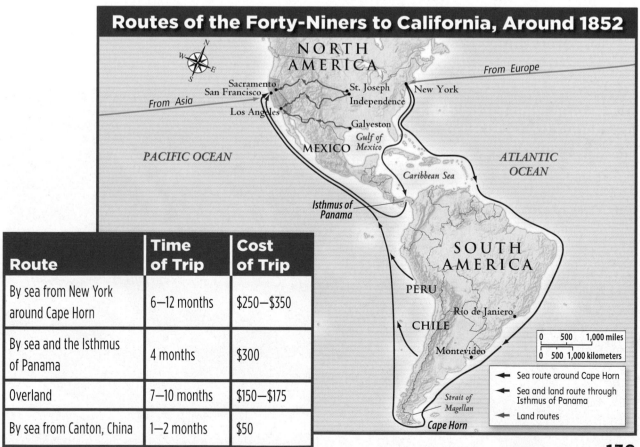

Routes of the Forty-Niners to California, Around 1852

Route	Time of Trip	Cost of Trip
By sea from New York around Cape Horn	6–12 months	$250–$350
By sea and the Isthmus of Panama	4 months	$300
Overland	7–10 months	$150–$175
By sea from Canton, China	1–2 months	$50

GOLD RUSH GLORY!

James Marshall discovered gold at Sutter's Mill on January 24, 1848. Sutter's Mill was a sawmill owned by John Sutter. It was in north central California. This discovery started the California Gold Rush.

More than 300,000 people went to California to find gold. They were men and women of all races and ages. They came by land and sea. Some people got very rich. Some lost everything. —*Lisa Jo Rudy*

▲ **Sutter's Mill in 1852**

Corbis

▼**People mine for gold in California during the Gold Rush.**

Bettmann/Corbis

James Beckwourth

James Beckwourth was born in Virginia in 1798. His mother was a slave. Beckwourth lived with the Crow and Blackfoot Indians in his early life. He was one of the few African American men in the Gold Rush. He was the only one to record his story.

After he got to California, he saw a gap through the Sierra Nevada mountains. He hoped this was a safe and easy way to cross the Sierras. Then it could be a new trade route.

Beckwourth led a group to explore the gap. Finally, they came to the eastern slope of the Sierras!

The Beckwourth Pass opened in 1851. The pass still has his name.

John Charles Fremont

John Charles Fremont was born in Georgia in 1813. He left home early, and went into the army.

In 1842, Fremont led two expeditions to the West. He discovered new routes to Oregon. People named him the Great Pathfinder.

In 1850, Fremont became a senator from the new state of California. In 1856, he tried to be President of the United States. He lost the election. After the Civil War, he became governor of Arizona. However, he did not do a good job. He had no money when he died. But he had changed the American West forever.

Fremont plants a U.S. flag on the Colorado Rockies, 1842 ▶

Sequence Writing Frame

Use the Writing Frame to orally summarize "Gold Rush Glory!"

The California Gold Rush inspired a lot of people to go west. One of them was James Beckwourth.

James Beckwourth's life **began** in _____.

His mother _____.

Early in life _____.

One day Beckwourth saw _____

_____.

The next spring, _____.

Finally, they came to _____.

In 1851, _____.

Today, the pass still has his name.

Use the Writing Frame to write the summary on another sheet of paper. Be sure to include **bold** signal words. Keep this as a model of this Text Structure.

Critical Thinking

1 Sleek, fast ships with many sails were called _____.

   A. clipper ships

   B. cargo ships

   C. forty-niner ships

2 Point to the sentence in "They Found Gold!" that helps you understand why people were called forty-niners.

3 Find the paragraph in "Gold Rush Glory!" that explains how John Charles Fremont received the name the Great Pathfinder.

4 Study the chart on page 139. With a partner, explain which route you think is the best way from New York to California.

Charts organize information and make it easy to remember.

Digital Learning

For a list of links and activities that relate to this History/Social Science standard, visit the California Treasures Web site at www.macmillanmh.com to access the Content Readers resources. Have students read the Biography "James Beckwourth."

CALIFORNIA BECOMES A STATE

The Mexican War ended in 1848. California was now a part of the United States, but it was not a state. The United States government in Washington, D.C., chose military governors. The people of California could not vote or choose their leaders. The old Mexican laws were still used. There was no court system.

This system worked while California was a rancho economy. However, everything changed once gold was discovered.

Thousands of people from all over the world came because of the Gold Rush. Mining camps and towns formed. The new arrivals in California wanted to make their own laws. Each mining area made and enforced its own rules. These different rules were confusing and often unfair.

▲ General Bennett F. Riley was the last military governor of California.

General Bennett F. Riley was the last military governor. He knew that he must act or people would be in trouble. He asked Californians to choose **delegates**, or people who would represent them. The delegates came to a **convention**, or meeting, at Colton Hall in Monterey. This meeting was the first step in writing a **constitution**. A constitution is a plan of government. The constitution would decide the size of California and the rights of its citizens.

The delegates decided to ask for statehood. They also decided that California was to be a free state. This meant that California did not allow slavery. The delegates also decided that the Sierra Nevada and the Colorado River were the eastern boundaries of California.

On September 9, 1850, California became the 31st state in the nation. Now, people celebrate that date each year as Admission Day.

The new state government chose the city of San Jose as its capital, or government center. But the capital moved to three other cities after that. Finally, Sacramento became the permanent capital in 1954.

The new state government was different from the earlier governments. During the Spanish and Mexican periods, the governor of California was appointed. The governor of the state of California was elected.

This room in Colton Hall, Monterey, is where delegates met to discuss California's constitution.

145

Biddy Mason

Bridget "Biddy" Mason was born August 15, 1818, in Mississippi. She was born a slave on a plantation owned by Robert and Rebecca Smith. Mason had three daughters, Ellen, Ann, and Harriet.

In 1847, Robert Smith joined the Mormon Church. He decided to move his family across the United States to the Utah Territory. It was a 2,000-mile trip. Biddy Mason and her daughters went along, too. Mason's job was to herd the cattle. She was also in charge of cooking. Of course, she took care of her own children.

▲ **Bridget (Biddy) Mason**

In 1851, Smith moved again. This time, he went to San Bernardino, California. Brigham Young, the founder of the Mormon Church, was starting a community there.

Smith probably did not know that California was a free state. That is, slavery was against the law.

In California, Mason learned about the law against slavery. She went to the court. She explained that she was a slave and this was against state law. In 1856 the California courts made Mason a free woman.

Corbis

Enslaved people picking cotton on a plantation in the South, early 1800s

Mason left Smith's house. She moved to Los Angeles with her daughters. There she became a nurse and midwife (a person who helps women give birth). Mason worked hard and saved her money.

She had enough money to buy land ten years after she was free. She was one of the first black women to buy property in Los Angeles.

In 1884, Mason sold part of her land. She made a good profit. She put up a building on the rest of the land and rented out space to businesses. Then she continued to make money in real estate. Mason had made a fortune by the time she died! Her grandson, Robert Curry Owens, was a real estate developer and politician. He became one of the richest men in Los Angeles.

Golden State Mutual Insurance Records, Collection 1434 box 41 Biddy Mason House, 1844

▲ **Biddy Mason's home, photographed in the 1870s**

Mason also gave money to charities and gave food and shelter to people in need. People loved Mason so much they built a special memorial in her honor in 1989. —*Lisa Jo Rudy*

▼**A memorial wall in Los Angeles honors Biddy Mason.**

Peter Bennett/CaliforniaStockPhoto

Problem/Solution Writing Frame

Use the Writing Frame to orally summarize "California Becomes a State."

In 1848, California was a part of the United States. But it was not

a state. **This was a problem because** _____

_____ .

After the war, old Mexican laws _____ .

To solve this problem, General Riley asked Californians to _____

_____ .

The delegates had to make important decisions. **The result** was

that they asked the U. S. Congress to make California _____

_____ .

On September 9, 1850, California became the 31st state in the nation.

Use the Writing Frame to write the summary on another sheet of paper. Be sure to include the **bold** signal words. Keep this as a model of this Text Structure.

Critical Thinking

1 A _____ is a plan of government.

   A. delegate

   B. convention

   C. constitution

2 Find the sentence in "Biddy Mason" that explains what a midwife is.

3 Point to the place in "California Becomes a State" that mentions an important difference between the new state government of California and governments during the Spanish and Mexican periods.

4 Select your favorite photo from "Biddy Mason." Orally create a new caption for it. Discuss your new caption with a partner.

Captions give information about a photograph.

Digital Learning

For a list of links and activities that relate to this History/Social Science standard, visit the California Treasures Web site at www.macmillanmh.com to access the Content Readers resources. Have students view "Becoming a State."

THE PONY EXPRESS

California's population grew rapidly in the 1850s. The people came far from the eastern United States. News, mail, supplies, and people took months to reach the West Coast. California needed better **communication** with the rest of the country. Communication is the exchange of information between people.

To speed up the mail, the U.S. government hired **stagecoach** companies. A stagecoach is a carriage pulled by a team of horses. Stagecoaches stopped at stations on their routes to change horses.

Stagecoaches provided faster **transportation** than wagon trains. Transportation is the movement of people and goods. A stagecoach from the Overland Mail Service took three weeks to travel 2,800 miles from Missouri to San Francisco.

On April 13, 1860, Billy Hamilton made the first delivery for the Pony Express. The Pony Express was the fastest mail service to California at the time. It was set up like a relay race. Each rider passed a bag of mail to the rider waiting ahead of him. The riders traveled day and night.

Each rider had a regular route separated by stations. A rider started from a station with a mail bag and galloped 10 to 15 miles to the next station. Then the rider would change to a new horse and ride to the next station. A new rider took over after about eight stations, or 80 to 100 miles. At the end of a route, a rider ate and slept at the station house until it was time to make the return trip.

The Pony Express mail service lasted only 18 months. A new technology replaced it—the telegraph.

The telegraph allowed Californians to communicate in seconds instead of weeks or days. The telegraph used electricity to send messages. Samuel F. B. Morse, who developed the first telegraph in 1836, designed a code to send messages. Morse's code uses patterns of dots and dashes for each letter of the alphabet.

By 1861 telegraph lines were strung on poles from coast to coast. The Western Union Telegraph Company owned most of the lines.

A coast-to-coast telegraph system was completed on October 24, 1861. The Pony Express ended soon after.

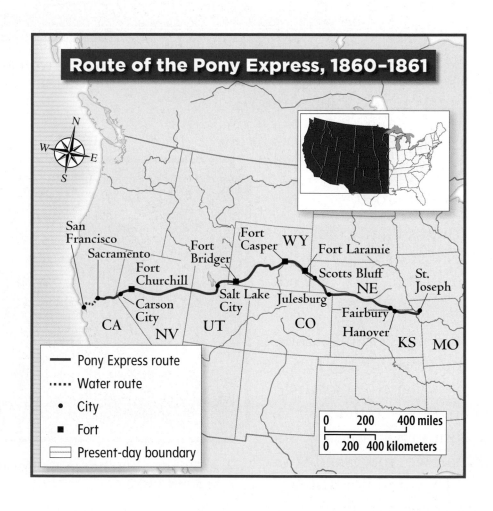

Route of the Pony Express, 1860–1861

San Francisco
Sacramento
Fort Churchill
Carson City
CA
NV
Fort Bridger
Salt Lake City
UT
Fort Casper
WY
Fort Laramie
Scotts Bluff
NE
Julesburg
CO
Fairbury
Hanover
KS
St. Joseph
MO

Pony Express route
Water route
City
Fort
Present-day boundary

0   200   400 miles
0   200   400 kilometers

A Chinese-American Marriage

In the late 1800s a remarkable California family was started by a Chinese man and an American woman.

The Granger Collection

▲ **Chinese workers on the transcontinental railroad**

In 1871 Fong See left his village in China and went to Sacramento, California. He searched for his father, who had disappeared while he helped build the transcontinental railroad.

Letticie Pruett's family crossed America in a covered wagon at about the same time. They settled in Oregon.

Fong See did not find his father, but he did find work. By the late 1890s, Fong See owned a clothing factory. Meanwhile, Letticie left home and went to Sacramento. She went to Chinatown and asked Fong See for a job. He hired her. Later, they decided to get married.

The Granger Collection

▲ **A Chinese butcher in California, around 1900**

In the 1890s it was against the law in California and many other states for Chinese and white people to marry. Chinese people could not own property or be citizens. They could no longer immigrate to the United States.

A lawyer helped Fong See and Letticie write a marriage contract. They married and moved to Los Angeles. There they raised five children. They ran five antique stores, too. Fong See became the first Chinese person in the United States to own a car. He even sold props to the new movie industry.

Fong See and Letticie married and were successful, but the laws did not change. Their four sons chose to marry Caucasian women. They had to go to Mexico to marry.

The laws did not change for a long time. Similar laws made life difficult for African Americans and Native Americans.

Finally, in 1965 mixed-race marriages became legal in the United States. Today it is common for people of different races and cultures to marry. —*Lisa Jo Rudy*

Bettmann/Corbis

▲ **It was common to treat the Chinese unfairly.**

Michael Buckner/Getty Images

▲ **Author Lisa See is the great-granddaughter of Fong See and Letticie See.**

Nick White/Digital Vision/Getty Images

▲ **Diverse families are common today.**

Sequence Writing Frame

Use the Writing Frame to orally summarize "A Chinese-American Marriage."

In the late 1800s a remarkable California family was started by a Chinese man and an American woman.

In 1871, Fong See _____ .

By the late 1890's Fong See _____ .

Meanwhile, Letticie _____ .

She went to _____ .

After Fong See hired her they _____ . **In 1890**

it was _____

_____ .

However, they married and moved to Los Angeles. Next, they _____

_____ .

The laws that made life difficult for Fong See, Letticie, and their

children did not change for a long time. **Finally**, in 1965 _____

_____ .

Use the Writing Frame to write the summary on another sheet of paper. Be sure to include the **bold** signal words. Keep this as a model of this Text Structure.

Critical Thinking

1 _____ is the movement of people and goods.

    A. Communication

    B. Stagecoach

    C. Transportation

2 Locate the name of the technology in "The Pony Express" that replaced the pony express.

3 Find the text in "A Chinese-American Marriage" that explains the laws against Chinese people in the 1890s.

4 Look at the map on page 151. Discuss the route of the Pony Express with a partner.

> Labels identify cities, states, rivers, or other land features.

Digital Learning

For a list of links and activities that relate to this History/Social Science standard, visit the California Treasures Web site at www.macmillanmh.com to access the Content Readers resources. Have students view "A Growing State."

LAND OF OPPORTUNITY

In the late 1800s, many people came to California for a better life for their families. Some came to escape harsh conditions. Others came to look for gold or jobs on railroads and farms.

Migration is a large movement of people from one place to another. People who lived in other parts of the United States moved to California. Others came from around the world. People who move to a new country are called **immigrants**.

Immigrants came to California to escape poverty or wars at home. Some saw newspaper ads for jobs. In 1913 a farmer advertised for people to help with a harvest. His ad brought workers from 27 different countries.

Many immigrants to California had the chance to earn money on farms. Some newcomers bought their own land. Others went to California's cities to live.

Immigrants from Russia, Poland, and Korea settled in such places as Los Angeles, San Francisco, and San Diego. They worked in factories, in restaurants, and on boats as fishermen.

In the middle 1920s, two young immigrants were giants in the film industry in Hollywood. They were Samuel Goldwyn from Poland and Louis B. Mayer from Russia. Metro-Goldwyn-Mayer, which has their names, (MGM) became one of Hollywood's biggest film studios.

Many immigrants to California came through Angel Island.

Immigrants who came from the same country had a common culture. Members of some immigrant groups settled together in neighborhoods in large cities. Mexican immigrants created their own communities within cities. Spanish was spoken in these neighborhoods, called **barrios**.

Immigrant communities also formed **mutual aid societies** to support new arrivals from their homelands. These organizations helped new immigrants find homes and jobs. The Mexican mutual aid societies were called **mutualistas**.

Some immigrant groups started their own towns. German immigrants started the city of Anaheim in 1857. They worked together on farms and shared the profits.

Competition for jobs and differences in culture often led to feelings of dislike, or **prejudice**, against immigrants. Some people treated immigrants unfairly. This kind of unfair treatment is called discrimination. Many immigrant communities in California worked to defend their members from discrimination and prejudice.

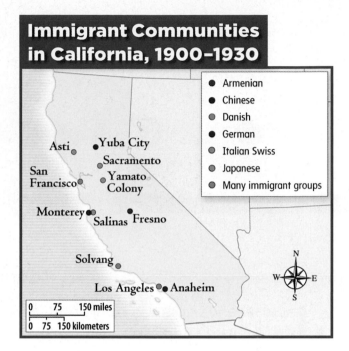

Immigrant Communities in California, 1900–1930

- Armenian
- Chinese
- Danish
- German
- Italian Swiss
- Japanese
- Many immigrant groups

Asti · Yuba City · Sacramento · San Francisco · Yamato Colony · Monterey · Salinas · Fresno · Solvang · Los Angeles · Anaheim

0   75   150 miles
0   75   150 kilometers

Immigrants soon became a large part of the California workforce. They also brought their kinds of music, dance, food, and celebrations. Immigrants made California a richer and more diverse place.

Japanese immigrant Kenju Ikuta showed that rice could be a California cash crop. Many rice farms were started in Northern California as a result. Gaetano Merola came to California from Italy in 1921. He started the San Francisco Opera two years later.

Manzanar

Corbis

U.S. ships at Pearl Harbor after the attack of December 7, 1941

Japanese war planes bombed U.S. planes and ships at Pearl Harbor, Hawaii on December 7, 1941. The attack destroyed nine ships. It also destroyed 188 aircraft. More than 4,000 Americans were hurt or killed. The United States immediately entered World War II.

The United States believed that the Japanese were planning a larger attack. President Franklin Roosevelt worried that Japanese Americans might help the Japanese government. Some people thought that Japanese Americans in California were spies for the enemy.

President Roosevelt approved a plan to protect the United States from Japanese spies. The plan gave army commanders the power to collect all Japanese and Japanese American people on the West Coast of the United States. All of these people, even American citizens, had to leave or else live in war relocation centers.

▼ **This notice ordered Japanese and Japanese Americans to war relocation centers.**

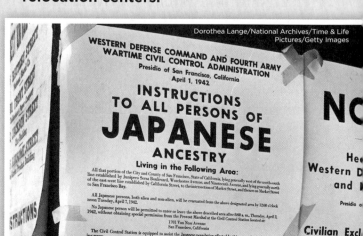

Dorothea Lange/National Archives/Time & Life Pictures/Getty Images

158

The entrance to Manzanar. Barracks are in the background.

▲ Families lived in crowded conditions. They had little privacy.

Mas Okui was 10 years old. He and his father and two brothers were sent to the Manzanar War Relocation Center. It was set on one square mile north of Los Angeles. For three years Okui lived in barracks. He put sheets between bunks for privacy.

Later, Okui became a schoolteacher. He gave tours of the site. Now, visitors can hear the stories of Okui and the 120,000 others who lived in war relocation centers.

The National Park Service opened a center for visitors to Manzanar. There, people can learn how Japanese and Japanese Americans lived there during the war. The purpose of the exhibit is to promote "dialogue on civil rights, democracy, and freedom."

Okui says, "What Manzanar should do is say to people, 'We did this. These people were cruelly treated. And I hope it never happens again.'"

▼ This monument at the Manzanar cemetery has the words, "Monument for the Pacification of Spirits."

Cause/Effect Writing Frame

Use the Writing Frame to orally summarize "Land of Opportunity."

People came to California for **many reasons** at the end of the 1800s.

One reason was to escape _____

_____ .

Another reason was to get jobs they saw in _____ .

The land, climate, and economic growth in California gave **many**

immigrants the chance to earn _____

_____ .

Some people went to cities to work in _____

_____ .

Because immigrants from the same country shared a common

culture, they _____ .

Use the Writing Frame to write the summary on another sheet of paper. Be sure to include **bold** signal words. Keep this as a model of this Text Structure.

Critical Thinking

1 A large movement of people from one place to another is known as _____ .

    A. immigrants

    B. migration

    C. mutualistas

2 Point to the word in "Land of Opportunity" for hatred or unfair treatment of immigrants.

3 Locate the section in "Manzanar" that explains why President Roosevelt approved war relocation centers.

4 Review the map on page 157 with a partner. Discuss the cities where immigrant groups settled. Are more of these cities located on the coast or inland?

> A key or legend helps you interpret the colors or special symbols on a map.

Digital Learning

For a list of links and activities that relate to this History/Social Science standard, visit the California Treasures Web site at www.macmillanmh.com to access the Content Readers resources. Have students view the Field Trip "San Francisco's Chinatown."

SOUTHERN CALIFORNIA GROWS

The population growth of the 1800s mainly affected the areas where gold was found in Northern California. Soon, railroads, industry, oil, and Hollywood brought millions of new people to Southern California. The population of Los Angeles grew from 11,000 to over a half million from 1880 to 1920.

One reason for the population boom, or increase, was the discovery of oil—"black gold." In 1893, Edward Doheny saw that the back of a wagon was filled with sticky dark soil. Doheny and a partner bought the land and drilled down until they struck oil. Then they built an oil **derrick** above the place. A derrick is a tower built over a drill site to hold a drill. It brings oil to the surface. Soon people from around the country moved to Southern California to find oil and make money.

At this time railroads began using oil for fuel instead of coal. Cars powered by gasoline (an oil product) were becoming popular. The fuel needed to be **refined**, or improved, for cars to use oil. In the 1920s, oil refining became California's biggest industry. More oil was exported from Los Angeles than from any other port in the world.

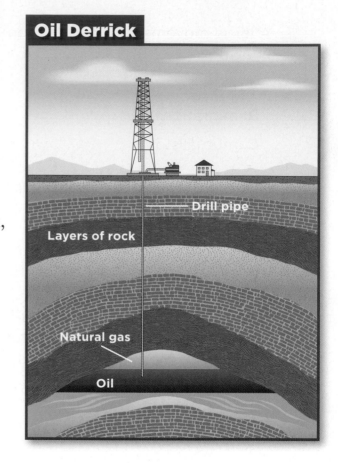

Oil Derrick

Drill pipe

Layers of rock

Natural gas

Oil

To support its growing population, Los Angeles needed to ship supplies in and ship products out. In 1907 the Port of Los Angeles opened. The port was the first stop in California for all ships from Europe, the eastern United States, and Central and South America. By the middle 1920s, Los Angeles was the busiest port in the western United States. It was a new center of trade.

Los Angeles was outgrowing its water supply. In 1890 William Mulholland became head of the Los Angeles water department. Mulholland's solution was to build an **aqueduct** to bring water to the city. An aqueduct is a large pipe that carries water over a long distance. The Los Angeles Aqueduct went 200 miles, from the Owens River to Los Angeles. The aqueduct supplied water to farms and the people of Los Angeles. With no more river flowing into it, however, Owens Lake dried up. Owens Valley farmlands suffered. By 1930 most of the farmers and ranchers in the Owens Valley sold their land and water rights to the city.

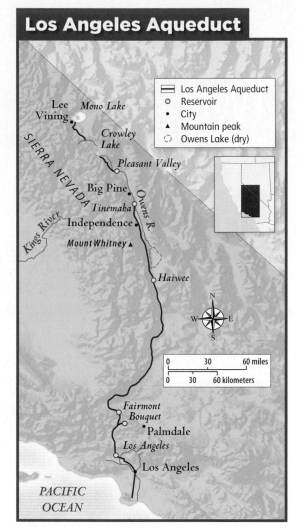

Los Angeles Aqueduct

- ▭ Los Angeles Aqueduct
- ○ Reservoir
- ● City
- ▲ Mountain peak
- ◌ Owens Lake (dry)

Lee Vining
Mono Lake
Crowley Lake
Pleasant Valley
SIERRA NEVADA
Big Pine
Owens R.
Tinemaha
Independence
Kings River
Mount Whitney ▲
Haiwee
Fairmont
Bouquet
Palmdale
Los Angeles
Los Angeles
PACIFIC OCEAN

0   30   60 miles
0   30   60 kilometers

▼ The Los Angeles Aqueduct opened on November 5, 1913.

Two California Photographers

▲ Dorothea Lange

▲ Ansel Adams

Oakland Museum of California

The Bancroft Library

Dorothea Lange

Dorothea Lange was born in Hoboken, New Jersey, in 1895. Lange learned photography in New York City. Later she moved to California to be a professional photographer.

The Great Depression came in 1929. Many people did not have homes or jobs. Lange took pictures of these poor people. One of her pictures became famous. It was called *The Migrant Mother*.

In 1940 Lange was the first woman to win an important prize for photography. She photographed Japanese Americans who were held in camps by the U.S. government during World War II.

Many people know Lange's work today. Her work is in museums around the world. You can see *The Migrant Mother* on a postage stamp.

Library of Congress

▲ *The Migrant Mother* is a photograph by Lange.

▼ Lange photographed a Japanese American family held by the U.S. government during World War II.

Dorothea Lange/National Archives/ Time Life Pictures/Getty Images

Ansel Adams

Ansel Adams was born in San Francisco in 1902. Adams loved the natural beauty of Yosemite National Park when he vacationed there with his family. He was 14 years old. He also loved to climb mountains. He began to develop his method of photographing natural landscapes.

Adams became interested in saving the wilderness. His photographs showed how national parks looked before humans arrived.

Adams also photographed people and buildings. He took pictures of Japanese Americans held in camps, such as Manzanar, during World War II. Later, he worked with Dorothea Lange to photograph a shipyard in Richmond, California.

Ansel Adams is one of America's best-loved photographers. He won many prizes and his work is shown around the world. —*Lisa Jo Rudy*

Ansel Adams Publishing Rights Trust/Corbis

▲ *Moon and Half Dome*, Yosemite National Park, a photograph by Adams

▼ Adams photographed this Japanese family held in a camp.

Library of Congress

165

Compare/Contrast Writing Frame

**Use the Writing Frame to orally summarize
"Two California Photographers."**

Dorothea Lange and Ansel Adams **were alike because** they were both

_____ .

In addition, **they both** lived in _____ .

In some ways, however, _____ and

_____ **were different**. Lange was born in

_____ ,

while Adams was born in _____ .

Another difference was their work. Adams developed a method for

_____ .

However, during World War II, **both** photographers took photos of

_____ .

Lange and Adams also worked together to photograph a _____

_____ .

Use the Writing Frame to write the summary on another sheet of
paper. Be sure to include the **bold** signal words. Keep this as a
model of this Text Structure.

Critical Thinking

1 A large pipe that carries water over a long distance is an
_____ .

    A. port

    B. derrick

    C. aqueduct

2 Locate the sentence in "Southern California Grows" that tells what *refined* means.

3 Reread the paragraph in "Two California Photographers" that explains what happened when the Great Depression came.

Diagrams provide information that may not appear in the text.

4 Look at the diagram on page 162. Discuss with a partner how the diagram supports the text.

Digital Learning

For a list of links and activities that relate to this History/Social Science standard, visit the California Treasures Web site at www.macmillanmh.com to access the Content Readers resources. Have students read the Biography "Ansel Adams."

OUR GOVERNMENT

The U.S. Constitution was written over 200 years ago. It explains the role of the **federal**, or national, government in our country. The Constitution says that the government has three branches, or parts. Each branch has a job to do. Each branch also has some power over the other branches. This prevents any one branch from gaining too much power. The Constitution also limits the responsibility of the federal government. This is because it gives a lot of responsibility to each of our country's 50 states.

Branches of the Federal Government

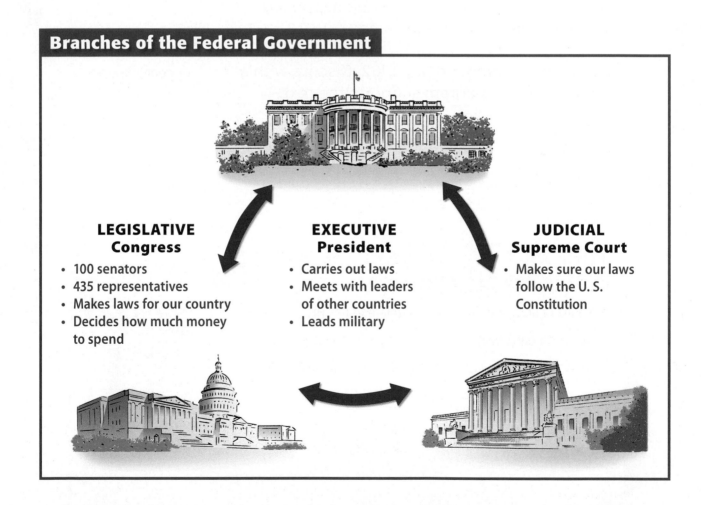

LEGISLATIVE
Congress

- 100 senators
- 435 representatives
- Makes laws for our country
- Decides how much money to spend

EXECUTIVE
President

- Carries out laws
- Meets with leaders of other countries
- Leads military

JUDICIAL
Supreme Court

- Makes sure our laws follow the U. S. Constitution

The **legislative branch**, or Congress, is the part of government that makes laws. It includes the Senate and the House of Representatives. Citizens elect senators and representatives to serve terms in Congress. Every state sends two senators to Congress. The number of representatives for each state depends on the state's population. States with greater populations have more representatives. California has 53 representatives. This is more than any other state.

Members of Congress meet in the Capitol to discuss issues and make new laws each year. They also help decide how much money to spend.

The **executive branch** carries out the laws. The President leads this branch. The President is also commander in chief of the U. S. military.

The **judicial branch** includes all the federal courts. These courts make sure everyone follows the laws. The Supreme Court is the highest court in the country. It decides if new laws passed by Congress and approved by the President agree with the Constitution. This is how the judicial branch checks the powers of the legislative and executive branches.

The California Constitution was written in 1849. It was modeled on the U. S. Constitution. Both constitutions divide the government into three branches. Both have a written list of people's rights, such as the freedom of speech and of religion. The California Constitution has changed a little over the years.

The U. S. Constitution applies to all of the citizens of our country. The California Constitution applies only to Californians. Also, the California Constitution is longer. Parts of it explain the jobs of the state government.

America's Grand Plan

On September 17, 1787, thirty-nine men put their names on one of history's most important documents: the Constitution of the United States of America. For four months in Philadelphia, Pennsylvania, they discussed the best way the federal government could work. Finally, they signed the document that is the grand plan for our government.

The U.S. Constitution divides power between the legislative, judicial, and executive branches of the federal government. It also divides powers between the national and state governments. Only some powers are given to the federal government. The states get all the other powers.

▲ **The Preamble of the U.S. Constitution**

George Washington and others sign the Constitution, September 17, 1787. ▶

California's Constitution

The U.S. Constitution allows states to have their own constitutions. State constitutions allow states to take care of their own needs. California's constitution makes a plan for the state's government and its education system. It tells the state how to collect taxes and spend tax money. The California state constitution includes ways to protect the state's ocean resources.

We Celebrate

In 2004 President George W. Bush signed a law that officially established September 17 as Constitution Day. The law requires all public schools on September 17 to discuss the Constitution. The first official celebration came in 2005. —*Martha Pickerill*

Bruce Burkhardt/Corbis

▲ **California State Capitol**

Charles Hess/National Constitution Center

▲ **Kids sign a copy of the Constitution at the National Constitution Center in Philadelphia.**

Who Has the Power?

This table shows how the Constitution divides some powers between the two levels of government. There are powers that are for one level only. There are also powers that the national and state governments share.

Power	Is It a National Government Power?	Is It a State Government Power?
Print money	Yes	No
Declare war	Yes	No
Give out drivers' licenses	No	Yes
Create public schools	No	Yes
Collect taxes	Yes	Yes
Build roads	Yes	Yes
Make laws	Yes	Yes

Description Writing Frame

**Use the Writing Frame to orally summarize
"Our Government."**

The government has three branches, or parts. Each branch
has a job to do.

For example, the legislative branch, or Congress, _____

_____ .

Congress includes the _____

_____ .

Another branch is the _____ .

It is led by the President, who is also _____

_____ .

The judicial branch of the federal government includes all the

federal courts. **For example**, _____

_____ .

The _____ checks the powers of
the legislative and executive branches.

Use the Writing Frame to write the summary on another sheet of
paper. Be sure to include the **bold** signal words. Keep this as a
model of this Text Structure.

Critical Thinking

1 The _____ branch carries out the laws.

   A. executive

   B. judicial

   C. legislative

2 Find the phrase in "Our Government" that explains the word *federal*.

3 Point to the place in "America's Grand Plan" that tells how the U.S. Constitution divides the responsibility between the federal and state governments.

4 Review the diagram on page 168. With a partner, discuss how it helps you understand the text.

A diagram uses pictures and labels to show how something works or is put together.

Digital Learning

For a list of links and activities that relate to this History/Social Science standard, visit the California Treasures Web site at www.macmillanmh.com to access the Content Readers resources. Have students view the Biography "Mariano Guadalupe Vallejo."

STATE GOVERNMENT

California's government is located in Sacramento, our state's capital. Like the federal government, California's government has three branches: legislative, executive, and judicial. Members of California's legislative and executive branches work in the state capitol building.

The state legislature consists of the 80-member State Assembly and the 40-member Senate. California's citizens elect members of the State Assembly for two-year terms. The citizens elect members of the Senate for four-year terms.

Assembly members can serve up to three terms. Senators serve up to two terms.

The California legislature studies and discusses **bills**. A bill is a suggestion for a new law. In 1996 the state legislature discussed a bill to decrease the size of many public elementary school classes. It would cost a lot of money to carry out this law. They voted in favor of the bill.

After most of the members of the Assembly and the Senate vote in favor of a bill, it goes to the governor for approval.

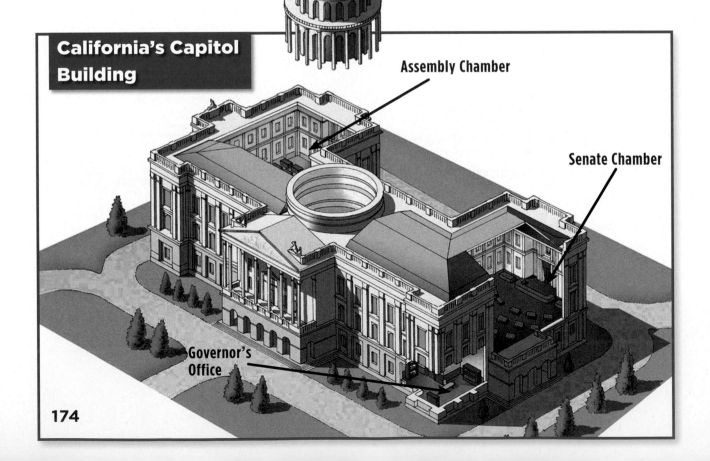

California's Capitol Building

Assembly Chamber

Senate Chamber

Governor's Office

The governor is the head of the state's executive branch. California's citizens elect governors. Governors can serve up to two four-year terms. The governor has the power to approve new laws by signing the bill. The governor can also **veto** the bill. A veto sends the bill back to the legislature.

The legislative branch then has the power to call a vote on the bill again. The bill becomes a law if two-thirds of the Assembly and Senate vote for it.

In 1996, Governor Pete Wilson signed the Class Size Reduction Program into law. It granted one billion dollars a year for more classrooms and teachers.

The judicial branch of the state government runs California's court system. The California judicial branch is only responsible for state law, not federal law.

California's highest court is the California Supreme Court. The governor appoints each of its seven judges. Citizens approve the judges in the next general election.

How a Bill Becomes a Law

1. Citizens develop an idea for a bill.

2. Members of the State Assembly or the Senate propose the bill.

3. The Assembly and the Senate vote to approve the bill.

yes   no

4. The governor signs or vetoes the bill.

5. Another vote can happen if the bill is vetoed. If more than two-thirds of the Assembly and the Senate vote to approve it, the bill becomes a law.

Driver's License

In airports, at stores, and many other places, a valid driver's license proves who you are.

Every state in the United States has its own laws about drivers' licenses. All states do not have the same age requirements. In California and most other states, you have to be 18 to get a full driver's license.

Every state requires drivers to take a written test and a driving test. The written test asks questions about the rules of the road. The driving test asks drivers to show that they can drive, back up, park, merge with traffic, obey traffic signs and signals, and react quickly.

Davd Young Wolff/PhotoEdit, Inc.

▲ **Most teenagers want to get a driver's license.**

Each state's license looks different, but they all have a photo and a special license number.

A National ID

States decide what is needed to get a drivers' license. This includes ways to prove the identity of someone applying for a license. The U.S. government does not issue a national identification card. Many other countries do.

Blend Images/SuperStock

▲ **All states require drivers to pass a driving test.**

The U.S. accepts state-issued drivers' licenses as proof of identity. All states require applicants for drivers' licenses to prove their identity and age. This is usually done with a birth certificate. Other documents are also accepted. Some applicants come from other countries. Then, a state employee may not have a way to make sure the information on documents provided is true.

Should requirements for drivers' licenses be the same in all states? Should the federal government list the information applicants must provide? Congress may pass new laws that affect how states issue drivers' licenses. One change may require applicants to prove they are in the United States legally. Another may require states to store driver's license information in a database that other states can use. Would this make a driver's license a national ID card? —*Lisa Jo Rudy*

Many countries, including England, have a national ID card.

Eyebyte/Alamy

▼ **Applicants for a driver's license**

Joe Raedle/Getty Images

Sequence Writing Frame

Use the Writing Frame to orally summarize "State Government."

The first step in a bill becoming a law is when citizens _____

_____ .

Next, members of the _____

_____ .

Then, the _____

_____ .

After that, the _____

_____ .

If the bill is vetoed, **then** _____

_____ .

If more than two-thirds of the Assembly and the Senate vote to

approve it, the bill **finally** _____ .

Use the Writing Frame to write the summary on another sheet of paper. Be sure to include the **bold** signal words. Keep this as a model of this Text Structure.

Critical Thinking

1 A _____ is a suggestion for a new law.

    A. veto

    B. bill

    C. assembly

2 Find the sentence in "State Government" that tells how long any governor can serve our state.

3 Find the text in "Driver's License" that tells how people applying for a driver's license prove age and identity.

4 Review the diagram on page 175. Discuss with a partner what happens if the governor vetoes a bill.

Diagrams provide information that may not appear in the text.

Digital Learning

For a list of links and activities that relate to this History/Social Science standard, visit the California Treasures Web site at www.macmillanmh.com to access the Content Readers resources. Have students view the Field Trip "Sacramento."

OUR LOCAL GOVERNMENT

City councils govern most cities and towns. A city council is the legislative branch of a city. It makes laws for the city. Most city councils have an odd number of members, usually five, seven, or nine. This is so a vote will not end in a tie.

Citizens elect council members. The city council will usually hire a city manager to run the daily affairs of the city in most California cities. The city manager's job is to make sure all the departments run smoothly. Look at the chart on this page to learn about the departments of local government.

Citizens elect a **mayor** to be the head of the local government in many cities. In San Francisco, the mayor appoints, or picks, people to run city departments.

Most of California's cities are not as large as San Francisco. In many smaller cities, such as Chico, voters do not directly elect the mayor. The city council chooses the mayor from among its members. The mayor then serves as the head of the city council.

States are divided into parts called counties. Every city and town in California is part of a larger **county**. California has 58 counties.

Departments of Local Government

 Fire Department provides ambulance, fire, and rescue services

 Police Department keeps citizens safe

 Environmental Services Department oversees garbage, recycling

 Parks and Recreation Department maintains parks

 Public Health Department helps citizens fight disease

 Finance Department collects taxes, handles city money

 Planning Department plans for city projects

 Building Inspection Department grants permits for new buildings, inspects plans

 Maintenance Department repairs streets, signs, traffic lights

▲ Californians of all backgrounds benefit from public education.

A board of supervisors governs a county. The board usually has five members. Each member represents a different district in the county.

A county provides many of the services of a local government. A county is also responsible for hospitals and courts. Courts make up the judicial branch of a local government.

Another kind of local government is tribal government. There are over 100 Native American reservations and rancherias in California. Each has its own **tribal government**.

A tribal government is like a city government. It provides many services, such as police, fire, and environmental protection. It operates schools, offers health care, and helps people find jobs.

Local governments do not always provide all the services people need. Sometimes a district is formed to manage a service that is outside a local government's responsibility. There are over 2,000 special districts in California. A board of directors runs each district. Special taxes pay for special districts. One service run by a special district is your school district.

California is divided into hundreds of school districts. A school board runs each district. The members of the school board and the state's education department make decisions about public education. California has the largest school system of any state. Nearly 6.5 million students attend public school in California.

In the Middle

Kennedy Frank likes being a sixth grader. "I have the privilege of changing classes," she told TFK. "And I'm getting new experiences by not having the same teacher all day."

Kennedy is 11 years old. She goes to Humboldt Park K–8 School in Milwaukee, Wisconsin. K–8 stands for "kindergarten through eighth grade." The school is part of a plan to change the way kids ages 10 through 15 are educated. More and more educators say no to middle schools for grades 6–8. They prefer K–8 schools.

Kevin J. Miyazaki/Redux

▲ **Younger kids can learn from older kids in K–8 schools.**

A Good Idea?

Middle schools were started in the 1970s to fix problems in traditional junior high schools. Junior high schools were for grades 7–9. Middle schools tried to help kids meet the challenges of high school. They offered classes and activities suited to grades 6–8. Middle schools added sixth graders. This helped prevent overcrowding in elementary schools.

Recent studies suggest that middle schools are not better than junior high schools. Psychologist Jaana Juvonen says sixth grade is a poor time to switch schools. Kids' minds and bodies are changing a lot at that age. They need to stay in the same school for a little longer.

The new middle schools affected how well students do. Between 1999 and 2004, elementary school students scored higher on reading and math tests. Middle school students made smaller gains in math and none in reading.

▲ Sixth graders might benefit from a K–8 school more than a middle school.

Some people believe that test scores cannot tell the whole story. Barry Fein, principal of Seth Low Intermediate School in New York City, believes in middle schools. He says middle schools offer students more classes, team sports, and clubs. Ryan Pallas, a seventh grader at Las Flores Middle School, in Rancho Santa Margarita, California, agrees. "I like being challenged," he says.

No Easy Answers

In California, issues like these are decided by individual school districts. Parents and students can choose a K–8 school or a middle school in the Capistrano Unified School District. "K–8 isn't a [magic] bullet," says Lois Anderson, a Capistrano assistant superintendent. "It won't make other challenges go away."

What's the Difference?

K-8		MIDDLE SCHOOL
► Many K–8 schools have labs, lockers, and other facilities similar to middle schools.	**Buildings**	► Middle schools are often larger. They may have big libraries and science labs.
► Older students in K–8 schools make solid gains in math and reading.	**Classes**	► Big middle schools have a richer selection of classes and more activities.
► Older kids can be leaders for younger students.	**Social Life**	► New school, new friends. For some, it is a fresh start. Others do not like being the youngest.

183

Problem/Solution Writing Frame

Use the Writing Frame to orally summarize "In the Middle."

Many school districts say no to middle schools for grades 6–8. They prefer K–8 schools.

The problem is that sixth grade is _____

_____

_____ .

According to psychologist Jaana Juvonen, **this problem**

happened because _____

_____

_____ .

To help solve this problem, some school districts allow parents

and students to _____

_____

_____ .

Use the Writing Frame to write the summary on another sheet of paper. Be sure to include the **bold** signal words. Keep this as a model of this Text Structure.

Critical Thinking

1. A city council is the _____ branch of a city.

   A. legislative

   B. executive

   C. judicial

2. Find the sentences in "Our Local Government" that explain tribal government.

3. Locate the section in "In the Middle" that describes the effect middle schools had on how well students do.

4. Review the chart on page 183. Do you want to go to a middle school or a K–8 school? Discuss this with a partner.

A chart has columns and rows. You read down the columns on some charts. You read across rows on other charts.

Digital Learning

For a list of links and activities that relate to this History/Social Science standard, visit the California Treasures Web site at www.macmillanmh.com to access the Content Readers resources. Have students view the Biography "Heather Fong."

Illustration Acknowledgements

7, 13: Argosy Publishing. 18: Tom Leonard. 30, 49, 60: Sam Tomasello. 162: Steve Stankiewicz. 168: Min Jae Hong. 174: Inklink. 175: Kenneth Batelman. 180: Rob Schuster

Photography Acknowledgements

All photos for Macmillan/McGraw-Hill except as noted below:

Cover: James Randklev/CORBIS. 6: Daryl Benson/Masterfile. 12: DK Limited/CORBIS. 13: BananaStock/PunchStock. 18: Siede Preis/Getty Images. 25: (tr) Yoav Levy/Phototake; (bcl) NASA JSC/Getty Images. 31: Phil Schermeister/CORBIS. 36: (b) Royalty-free/CORBIS; (br) Ian Rose/Frank Lane Picture Agency/CORBIS. 37: (cl) Joe McDonald/CORBIS; (bc) Steve Kaufman/Peter Arnold Inc.; (cr) Robert W. Ginn/PhotoEdit; (br) Eye of Science/Photo Researchers. 42: AGE Fotostock/SuperStock. 43: Robert Pickett/CORBIS; (br) Stockbyte. 54: (b) Frank Krahmer/Zefa/CORBIS; (inset) Frank Krahmer/Zefa/CORBIS. 55: (bl) Mervyn Rees/Alamy; (br) Anup Shah/Taxi/Getty Images; (b) Raymond Gehman/CORBIS. 60: Hans Pfletschinger/Peter Arnold Inc. 61: George D. Lepp/CORBIS. 66: Stephen Dalton/NHPA. 67: (tr) Kevin Schafer/CORBIS; (b) Klaus Nigge/NGS Images/Getty Images. 73: (cr) Roland Birke/Peter Arnold Inc.; (tcr) Custom Medical Stock Photo/Alamy; (br) PHOTOTAKE Inc./Alamy. 78: (t to b) TH Foto-Werbung/Photo Researchers; Wally Eberhart/Visuals Unlimited; Ben Johnson/Photo Researchers; Andy Crawford/DK Images; Randy Allbritton/Getty Images; Wally Eberhart/Visuals Unlimited; Image Farm Inc./Alamy; Lawrence Lawry/Photo Researchers. 79: (cr) Andrew J. Martinez/Photo Researchers; (br) Joyce Photographics/Photo Researchers; (b) Brad Lewis/Visuals Unlimited; (bl) Joyce Photographics/Photo Researchers; (cl) Creatas/PunchStock. 84: Royalty-free/CORBIS. 85: Carmel Studios/SuperStock. 90: (tr) Tony Arruza/CORBIS; (b) AGE Fotostock/SuperStock. 91: Joel W. Rogers/CORBIS. 108: (b) Gibson Stock Photography; (cr) Theo Allofs/Visuals Unlimited. 115: John Hudson/The Field Museum. 121: (b) Gary Crabbe/Enlightened Images; (tcr) Robert Holmes/CORBIS. 133: Brian A. Vikander/CORBIS. 138: Dave G. Houser/CORBIS. 144: Courtesy of the Bancroft Library, University of California, Berkeley. 145: Gary Moon. 156: Courtesy of State Museum Resource Center, California State Parks. 163: CORBIS. 181: Bill Aron/PhotoEdit Inc.